Point of Aim
Point of Impact

Jay Taylor

authorHOUSE®

AuthorHouse™
1663 Liberty Drive
Bloomington, IN 47403
www.authorhouse.com
Phone: 1-800-839-8640

© *2010 Jay Taylor. All rights reserved.*

No part of this book may be reproduced, stored in a retrieval system, or transmitted by any means without the written permission of the author.

First published by AuthorHouse 2/17/2010

ISBN: 978-1-4490-6208-8 (e)
ISBN: 978-1-4490-6206-4 (sc)
ISBN: 978-1-4490-6207-1 (hc)

Library of Congress Control Number: 2009913613

Printed in the United States of America
Bloomington, Indiana

This book is printed on acid-free paper.

Forty years is a long time for a thirteen-month span of your life to still affect you, but that is the case for many of us who served in Vietnam. On the surface most of us have moved on and become productive members of society. We have married, raised our families, and are now either retired or nearing retirement, and yet none of us will ever completely forget the events we endured those forty or so years ago. This book is for the wives and husbands who put up with our mood swings, our temper tantrums, our nightmares, and our unpredictability; for the children we raised who also had to endure our erratic behavior; and for the parents who, when we returned home, tried so hard to help but had no idea of what they were dealing with.

I would especially like to thank my very special wife. It was only with her help, support, and understanding that I have been able to succeed in life, and progress to the point where I could actually deal with my issues, and finally write this account of the time I spent in Vietnam as a Marine Corps Scout Sniper.

I owe a special thanks to Bill Martin and Chuck Butler. They furnished many of the pictures and much of the memorabilia. They also helped revive many old lost memories. I also would like to thank W.T. Maner and my two sons, Lee and Bobby, for never tiring of listening to my war stories.

I would like to recognize all of the individuals who served in the 7th Marine Scout Sniper Platoon, Bravo Company, and all of the individuals who served in Vietnam. Not all of the times were bad.

Jay Taylor

Table of Contents

Introduction: The Socialist Republic of Vietnam	ix
1. In the Beginning	1
2. Sniper School	6
3. Arriving in Country	10
4. Hill 55	14
5. My Tenure as an S-1 Office Pogue	22
6. Cpl Gang	25
7. Scout Sniper Platoon	28
8. First Kill	33
9. Bagging the Bush	36
10. The Gang	39
11. William L. Mott	42
12. Phantom Firefight	58
13. Friendly Fire	62
14. Kids and Kool-Aid	65
15. Heroes and Cowards	67
16. Hanna and the Worm	71
17. Bravo Company	75
18. My Gear	83
19. Tricks of the Trade	85
20. The New Lieutenant	97
21. What Are Friends For?	101
22. Our My Lai	104
23. Lt Heagerty and the Swamp	108
24. The Congressional Medal of Stupidity	112
25. Read the Signs	115
26. Partners	126
27. Olympic Shooter	131
28. Longest Confirmed Kill	133
29. Confirmed Kills	136
30. My First and Only Chopper Ride	140
31. Command Decisions	145
32. Politics	151
33. Bronze Star	153
34. Sniper Myths	156

35. The Old Woman and the House	160
36. The Perfect Bush	164
37. Leaving Country	171
38. Forty Years Later	185
39. Epilogue	193
References	194

Introduction: The Socialist Republic of Vietnam

With a land area of 204,788 square miles, Vietnam is slightly larger than the state of New Mexico. It is bordered by Cambodia, China, and Laos. Vietnam has over 2,000 miles of coastline including land on the Gulf of Thailand, the Gulf of Tonkin, and the South China Sea. Vietnam is 1,025 miles long, north to south, and 31 miles wide at its narrowest point. Vietnam ranges in elevation from sea level at the coastline to 10,300 feet above sea level at the highest mountain peak. The current population of Vietnam is over 86 million people.

In December of 1961 and at the request of South Vietnamese President Ngo Dinh Diem, President Kennedy dispatched military advisors to South Vietnam to help deal with the Viet Cong campaign. The communist-backed Viet Cong were fighting a guerilla war against the U.S.-backed South Vietnamese government, in an attempt to reunite the country under communist rule. By 1964, President Kennedy had increased the U.S. military presence in Vietnam from 800 to 16,000 personnel. In March of 1965, President Johnson sent the first U.S. combat forces to Vietnam.

The Vietnam War lasted longer than the Civil War, the First World War, and the Second World War put together. The United States spent 140 billion dollars and suffered over 58,000 American deaths and over 300,000 wounded. South Vietnam suffered 560,000 dead and 1,170,000 wounded. North Vietnam incurred 1,100,000 dead and 600,000 wounded. Nearly 2,000 Americans are still missing in action. Over 3 million American personnel served within the borders of South Vietnam, 7,484 of which were women.

I will be sixty years old in a few months. My Vietnam experience started over forty-two years ago. Since that time I have spent years trying to forget the details and events of what happened during that thirteen-month period of my life. I am sure time has clouded my memory.

Working as a Scout Sniper, I was attached to several different companies in the 7th Marine Regiment that were stationed throughout the 7th Marine TAOR (Tactical Area of Responsibility). I do not remember the names of all of the people I worked with, and in some cases I have taken my best guess at them. However, I can still picture many of their faces. Over the years I have talked with friends and other veterans about our experiences in Vietnam, and by doing so I have managed to keep some of those memories alive and intact. I have read some of the books currently on the market about Vietnam-era Scout Snipers, and although some are good, others contain some pretty hard-to-believe tales. Most of these books were not written by snipers. They were written by authors whose only goal was to make a profit, and many do not accurately reflect actual events. This book is my attempt to paint a more accurate picture of what being a sniper in Vietnam was like and at the very least, to tell my story and give some recognition to those I worked with.

Our story does not end with Vietnam. Many still struggle with the memories and the guilt. I do not claim to have killed large numbers of enemy soldiers while in Vietnam, but I was good at my job, and so were the others in our platoon. Being a sniper was like any type of big game hunting—our success was largely dependent on how much big game was in our hunting area. I was awarded the Bronze Star, a Navy Commendation, and a Meritorious Combat Promotion. My last seven months in country I had the pleasure of working with Bravo 1/7 on Hill 10 and Hill 65 where we were afforded plenty to opportunities to kill or be killed. Bravo's TAOR had plenty of big game in it.

1. In the Beginning

As a family we were not frequent church goers. Mom and Dad had both come from the South—Dad was a native of Arkansas and Mom was from Alabama—where they had been raised in religious families. My parents did a good job of teaching me right from wrong and instilling a good set of moral values, including teaching me the importance of the Ten Commandments. Little did I know how much the fifth commandment, "Thou shalt not kill," would come to haunt me later in life.

I grew up in the rural South Valley area of Albuquerque, New Mexico. My family lived on a two- acre mini farm which was located next door to Mr. Porter's twelve-acre apple orchard. Down the dirt road from us was a dairy farm, and across the road was Alhgrim's chicken farm. At the west end of the road was a twenty-acre field with a couple cottonwood trees and some sagebrush. There was a large prairie dog town in the field which made it a favorite hunting spot of mine. Mr. Bass owned a sixteen-acre field on the corner by the paved highway east of our place where he raised a few head of beef and grew alfalfa. Next to the field facing the paved highway was a country store and gas station that Mr. Bass also owned and operated. The school bus stop was located next to Mr. Bass's store.

When I was in grade school, I always made sure I got to the bus stop early so I could visit with Mr. Bass in his store. He had a small, clear plastic case on the counter with donuts in it. They cost a nickel each. Most of the time I had a nickel to buy a donut, but the times I didn't, all I had to do was stare at that case long enough and Mr. Bass would eventually say, "Go ahead, you can have one." What a grand old man he was.

Often after school, when the bus arrived back at Mr. Bass's store, my dog Missy would be waiting for me at the bus stop. Missy was a small, about thirty-five-pound, German shepherd–looking dog that Mom had brought home as a puppy when I was eight years old. Missy would stand there by the store, anxiously waiting for me to arrive. As soon as I got off the bus and headed for home, she would run circles around me, wagging her tail and barking. This could mean only one thing. She had a squirrel treed in Porter's apple orchard and it was now my job to shake or shoot it out for her.

Throughout my childhood I enjoyed hunting and fishing. Dad was not an avid hunter, but he did manage to take my brother and me deer and elk hunting a few times. I killed my first deer when I was thirteen years old. I always had a BB gun, and later a pellet gun which I used to hunt birds and squirrels in Porter's apple orchard and along the irrigation ditches. I would keep the sparrows I had shot and feed them to the old sow pig Mr. and Mrs. Porter had behind their house. I would pitch the sparrows into the old sow's pen, and she would catch them in midair and swallow them whole. At times I would forget and leave one of the sparrows in my pants pocket, and when Mom found the remains in her washing machine she would be very displeased with me to say the least.

My mom and I have always had a very close relationship. Being the younger of two boys, I spent more time with my mother while my older brother received the larger share of our dad's time. A great deal of Dad's work was for the Bureau of Indian Affairs, and it kept him away from home during the week. The majority of his jobs were on the Indian reservations in New Mexico and Arizona. When Jerry, my brother, was old enough, he often went with Dad while I stayed at home and helped Mom with the livestock and chores around the house.

Mom and Dad worked long hours in the family construction business, and by the time I was a teenager they had become moderately successful. Dad claimed his first thoroughbred racehorse in 1960, and from that time on we kept one or two broodmares at the farm. We raised their foals and raced them at the local tracks.

In the summertime I worked at the chicken farm across the road, and in the fall I picked apples for Mr. Porter. When September rolled around, I would sell popcorn and cokes at the state fair and during the horse racing meet. By the time I was 14 I had saved up enough money to buy a Remington 22 pump rifle and an old horse named Clyde. Clyde was a thoroughbred, and he was probably old enough to vote when I got him. You could count every rib in his body, and sitting on his back when he was trotting was like trying to ride a jack hammer, but he was mine. With Missy tagging along behind us, we could now ride up to the mesa to hunt the jackrabbits and cottontails that roamed the sagebrush flats.

In high school I participated in sports. I played football and wrestled. I graduated from High School in 1967 when I was seventeen years old. I had an opportunity to go to Adams State Collage on a wrestling scholarship, but at the time I felt I was entirely too intelligent for college.

Before joining the Marine Corps I knew I would probably wind up in Vietnam, and with only a high school education, I knew there was a strong possibility I would see combat. Like many others at the time, I thought something might happen, like the war ending or getting stationed in Germany, which would help me avoid combat duty or even going to Vietnam altogether. Like most young men I was a little concerned about how I would react in combat situations. Would I have the courage necessary to function and survive? Could I really take another person's life if I was placed in that situation? I was very naïve, and the thought of going to war was very frightening and yet fascinating at the same time.

I joined the Marine Corps in September 1967 just after my eighteenth birthday, which by the way did not make my mother the slightest bit happy. I actually went down to the courthouse the day after my birthday to join the army. I knew I would get drafted soon and jobs were hard to come by if you were classified 1-A like I was, so I thought I would just get it over with. I believed that this great country of ours guaranteed us our freedom and the right to pursue our happiness, and all that was asked from us in return was that we pay our taxes and fulfill our six-year military obligation. I only wanted to join for two years of active duty—I knew I did not want to make a career out of the military. The army told me they had no two-year program except the draft, and I was informed that if I volunteered for the draft I would have to wait at least six months before I would be called up. I didn't want to wait without a job for six more months.

The army recruiter then said, "Boy, if you are in that big of a hurry to join and you only want to join for two years then walk across the hall. I think the Marine Corps has a two-year plan." My stint in the Marine Corps thus started.

I made the short trip across the hall and promptly joined the Marine Corps. The recruiting officer could have been the poster marine. He was a powerfully built man who stood over six feet tall. His uniform did not have a wrinkle in it, and he had rows of ribbons on his chest. He tried to talk me into joining for four years, but I was set on just two years. I knew if I only joined for two years I would only do one tour in Vietnam.

I breezed right through the physical and other tests only to find out I was colorblind. The sergeant giving the test stamped *Failed* in big letters on my colorblind test, so I asked him if it meant they were not going to take me.

He replied, "Son, that means you are colorblind. We're damn sure gonna take ya, now move on down the line." I wondered why everyone called me "boy" and "son." I was going to be a Marine soon. Two weeks after walking across that hall I was shipped out to the San Diego, California, MCRD (Marine Corps recruit depot) for ten weeks of boot camp.

One of my first instructors in boot camp said something I never forgot. He said, "You pukes had better pay close attention because what we are about to teach you may someday save your life." He convinced me, and I did the best I could to stay alert and pay close attention in all of our classes.

During boot camp we were taught the basics about the Marine Corps and its history. We were taught how to march and how to shoot the M-14 rifle. We learned the simple basics of using a bayonet, knife fighting, and hand-to-hand combat. Upon the completion of our twelve-hour hand-to-hand training, our instructor informed us that we knew just enough to go to the nearest bar and get our asses kicked. I thought about his statement for a moment and decided he was right. Just because we were "badass marines" didn't mean we could let our mouths overload our abilities. Above all else we were in great physical condition. We were always running or marching or doing exercises. By the time I graduated from boot camp, my body weight had gone from a soft 170 pounds to 185 pounds in eight weeks, and it was all muscle.

We spent the last two weeks of boot camp at the rifle range. On the last day we shot for our marksmanship qualification scores. We shot from the standing, kneeling, and prone positions at ranges of 100 yards, 200 yards, 300 yards, and 500 yards. I never was any good from the kneeling position. In order to qualify as an expert marksman, we had to score a 220 or above out of a possible 250. I shot a 221, and the high score of our platoon was 227. I graduated from boot camp with a 0311 MOS (military occupational specialty), which was basic infantry rifleman. I would be a grunt—so much for getting assigned somewhere other than Vietnam.

After graduating from boot camp in early January 1968, we were sent to Camp Pendleton for four weeks of ITR (infantry training regiment). During ITR, one of our instructors was talking about ways to avoid booby traps when he made the statement, "If it didn't grow there, don't f—k with it." This would become my golden rule during my time in Nam.

Later on during one of our other classroom training sessions, a marine staff sergeant came into the class and talked to us about a new program the Marine Corps had started called the Scout Sniper Program. He explained that we would go thru four more weeks of schooling at Camp Pendleton, and upon completion of the course, we would have to qualify as experts on the range to get our 8541 Scout Sniper MOS. To be eligible for the course we needed to have shot expert at the rifle range during boot camp, and we would have to pass a physiological examination. When he had completed his presentation he asked for volunteers.

Well, being that I was in no hurry to get to Vietnam and I had qualified expert in boot camp, I raised my hand for the first time since I had joined the corps. The sergeant took me and fifteen other volunteers outside and asked us a few questions as a group. Did any of us smoke? They did not want smokers in the snipers. Did we think we could kill someone who was not pointing a gun at us? Did we all have 20/20 vision? We all quickly replied yes. He then informed us we had all passed the physiological exam. It was obvious the physiological part of that brief exam had not yet been entirely developed.

2. Sniper School

After ITR I was placed on guard duty for three weeks while I waited until the next Scout Sniper School started. Guard duty consisted of walking post at a few different locations around the base. My post was two new two-story barracks which were under construction. I patrolled on foot thru each of the barracks for eight hours, and then I had eight hours off. After a week of walking post, I got twenty-four hours off. I carried an M-14 rifle and three rounds of ammunition while on duty. It was an uneventful time, and it seemed like those three weeks dragged on forever.

Sniper school consisted of a combination of classroom work and many hours at the range. We were issued Remington 700s with 3x9 Redfield scopes. This was the same model rifle I would use in Vietnam. The scope had a built-in rangefinder that most of us never used while we were in Vietnam. The range finder was only good for 400 yards, though in some of the later scopes it was good up to 700 yards. The rifle came with an adjustable trigger which we normally set at eight to twelve ounces of pull and a bull barrel that was imbedded in fiberglass at the chamber. Bedding the chamber allowed the barrel to free float. You could wrap a dollar bill around the barrel and slide it all the way up to the chamber without it touching the stock. This was done for two reasons, first, so the barrel would vibrate the same each time a bullet traveled through it, and second, so if the wood stock warped a little, it would not create a pressure point on the barrel. As a barrel heats up, it may also warp a little. If anything was touching the barrel while the bullet was traveling through it, the barrel vibration would change, thus causing the flight path of the bullet to change.

We shot 308 caliber match ammunition. At the time the ammo was mainly made in one location—Lake City Army Ammunition Plant. The Lake City plant was located in Independence, Missouri.

It was located on a 4,000-acre government plot and was operated by Remington Arms. Match ammunition was made in lots, so the boxes would be marked "L.C." followed by the lot number. The manufacturer would run a limited amount of ammo through the production line, and then they would shut down the assembly line to recalibrate all of the equipment. After ensuring the accuracy, they would make another lot. Each time they did this they changed the lot number on the boxes. Each time the lot number changed we would re sight in or "re dope," as we called it, our rifles. Other than that, we never changed the dope on our rifle. We just held under or over the target depending on the range. During Sniper School my weapon was sighted in for 500 yards point of aim point of impact. In Nam I normally kept my rifle sighted in for 600 yards point of aim point of impact.

We were trained to use an infrared scope for nighttime shooting. An infrared scope consisted of two pieces of equipment. One was the scope which allowed us to see infrared light, and the other was the light that was mounted on top of the scope. The light projected a beam of infrared light like a flashlight, and it was undetectable with the human eye. When attached to a rifle it was a big and top-heavy unit. Training was the only time I ever used the infrared scope. In Nam we used the Starlight scope instead. The Starlight scope magnified the light from the moon and stars, thus allowing the user to see in the night.

The classroom work was extensive. We learned about our rifles and how the barrels were made. Similar to the ammo, the first rifles off the production line were the most accurate. We had classes about ballistics where we learned what made the bullet fly and how to gauge its flight path or trajectory. The twists in the lands and grooves (the grooves were cut inside the barrel in a spiral pattern, and the high, flat points between the grooves were called the lands) in the barrel caused the bullet to spin, and the spinning was what stabilized the bullet in flight. The further a bullet flew, the less it spun and the more unstable it became, until finally, it began to tumble. This was one of the reasons why at long ranges it was more difficult to keep tight bullet groups. Wind and other weather conditions could affect the flight path of a bullet as well. We were taught how to judge the wind speed and how to adjust for it. We were also taught how to estimate distances by the size of the target in the scope and by using maps.

We learned ways to conceal ourselves and how to build a hide. A hide was what the instructors called our place of concealment when we were set up and looking for the enemy. Snipers were deployed in two-man teams consisting of a team leader and a spotter, with the objective being to engage the enemy at long range and then flee before being discovered. For this reason the hide had to be large enough to conceal two snipers. I always worked with one or sometimes two partners who were an equal part of our success. My partner normally carried an M-16 rifle and a set of binoculars. At times he carried an M-14 rifle along with a Starlight scope for use at night. He was my partner, my spotter, and my protector, but he was not always my friend. We were taught to never walk on the top of a hill where we could be seen on the skyline by the enemy. We learned to always plan three routes of escape, although in Nam this was not always possible. Contrary to popular belief and the movies, we were taught never to hide in a tree, not that I needed to be told to stay out of trees. If detected by the enemy there was only one way out of a tree, and in addition trees provided very poor shooting positions. Another key was to never hide by or behind the only tree or rock on a hillside. These types of things were landmarks and the first places the enemy would look for the shooter—and they usually looked with mortars and small arms fire.

We were taught how to call in artillery so we could act as forward observers when the enemy force was too large for a two-man team to engage, or too far away for us to be effective with our 700. We were also taught to keep a log and record daily data, such as where we had been, where we had set up our hides, enemy activity, time of day, and data about shots we took, distance, and impact of the bullet. It did not take me long to quit doing this when I arrived in Nam. I guess I just never appreciated the importance of keeping a daily log. Right or wrong, I kept my notes in my head. I felt I had more important things to carry than a notebook and pen, like food, ammo, and water.

By the end of the sniper course, we were required to qualify on moving targets at five hundred yards. Each day at the range we practiced shooting at moving targets at a five-hundred-yard range.

The targets had an eighteen-inch bull's-eye, and they were carried by marines still in boot camp. They were down in the butts (the dirt mounds providing them safety) and carrying the targets taped to a long wooden two-inch by two-inch stick so the target stuck up above the butts. They would pace back and forth carrying the targets while we shot at them. At first we were intent on hitting the bull's-eye, which soon became a fairly easy task. Then one day while we were firing at the moving targets one of the guys noticed that when a bullet struck low on the target and hit the stick the target was taped to, the stick would be nearly knocked out of the hands of the poor recruit holding it. The impact of the bullet on the stick must have really stung their hands. That was a bad day for those recruits because from that point on we all tried to shoot the stick instead of the bull's-eye, and we could tell when one of us hit the stick because the target would almost drop out of sight and then pop back up. When the final day came and we shot for qualification scores, none of our group failed to qualify.

On 19 April 1968, I graduated from Scout Sniper School. There was no ceremony. On the last day of school and after having successfully qualified at the range, we were handed our graduation certificates and sent to our next duty station.

The marines who graduated from these classes were some of the early pioneers of what today has become a large sniper community involving all branches of the military. I would estimate there were only between 700 and 800 Marine Corps Scout Snipers in Vietnam during the entire course of the war, many of whom did not return home alive.

3. Arriving in Country

The first American soldier killed in the Vietnam War was Air Force TSgt Richard B. Fitzgibbon, Jr. He is listed by the U.S. Department of Defense as having a casualty date of June 8, 1956. His name was added to the Vietnam Memorial Wall on Memorial Day, 1999.

The first battlefield fatality was Specialist 4 James T. Davis, who was killed on December 22, 1961.

We departed California on April 25, 1968, en route to South Vietnam. We had a scheduled two-hour layover in Hawaii. While the plane was being refueled, we were allowed to exit the plane and wait in a section of the airport that had been roped off from the rest of the public areas. One of the guys I had been in sniper school with was from Hawaii. He was married and his wife had just had their first baby, and he had not seen his new son yet. He called his wife as soon as we got off the plane in hopes she and their son could get to the airport in time for them to be able to spend some time together. He really wanted a chance to hold his son for the first time, especially knowing that he was en route to Vietnam and might not ever get another chance. The officer in charge was aware of his situation and was willing to allow them some time together. Unfortunately, his wife and baby were unable to make it to the airport before we had to re-board the plane. Once we were all back onboard the plane and it had started to taxi out, the young marine spotted his wife holding their newborn son as she stood inside the airport at one of the windows. I saw a tear roll down his face; he had to be wondering if he was ever going to get to hold his son. It was a good thing we were all young, tough marines or there would not have been a dry eye on the plane. I learned later he did make it home on his R&R.

We were on our way to Okinawa, where we were held over for a few days to get processed for our trip to Nam. We did not get to see much of Okinawa because we were not allowed off base. We were confined to a small area of the base which consisted of the barracks, the supply depot, and the storage buildings. We packed all of our stateside gear in boxes for storage, and we were issued jungle boots, fatigues, and more travel papers. We could only take what we could pack in a duffel bag. Two days after arriving in Okinawa we were bussed back to the airport and boarded a plane to Vietnam. We had a saying: "What more can they do to us? Shave our heads and send us to Vietnam?"

We landed in Da Nang on the morning of May 4, 1968. The first thing that hit me as soon as I stepped off the plane was the heat and humidity. Immediately I noticed the mirages coming off the asphalt runways. We had been taught in sniper school how, on a still day, by sitting behind a shooter and using binoculars, a person could see the path of a bullet as it cut through mirages. There would be no problem seeing the bullet path over here. The mirages were very visible; they snaked their way up off the hot asphalt runways like smoke rising on a still day. The Da Nang airport was a very bustling place with helicopters and jets everywhere and people loading and unloading them. Everyone seemed to be in a hurry. We were rushed to one of the nearby metal buildings where we were divided into groups and assigned to different units. I and ten others were loaded into a deuce and a half (a 2 1/2 ton M35 cargo truck) that was bound for Hill 55, headquarters for the 7th Marine Regiment.

The 7th Marine Regiment was formed in 1917. They were called to duty in Vietnam in 1965 and preformed valiantly until the Regiment returned to the United States in September 1970.

The 7th Marine Regiment consisted of three battalions and a headquarters company. The 7th Marine Headquarters Company was located on Hill 55. Hill 55 was located seven miles southwest of Da Nang and was known as one of the most notorious area in I Corps. The 7th Marine Scout Snipers were a part of the regimental headquarters company. Each of the three battalions (1st, 2nd, and 3rd) consisted of a headquarters company and four rifle companies. They also had supporting elements: artillery batteries, tanks, Ontos tanks, an amtrac platoon, and mortars. First Battalion consisted of four rifle companies—Alpha, Bravo, Charlie, and Delta—2nd Battalion had Echo, Foxtrot, Golf, and Hotel, and 3rd Battalion had India, Kilo, Lima, and Mike. Each company consisted of three rifle platoons and a HQ platoon. At times a company also had a mortar squad or machine gun squad.

The company commander was a captain. Rifle platoons were commanded by a first or second lieutenant and a platoon sergeant. Each rifle squad had a squad leader and three fire teams consisting of three to four grunts. In all, a regiment consisted of 2,000 to 3,000 marines plus or minus.

From 1965 to 1969, the 7th Marine Regiment had 1,503 of its marines killed in action, and 85 U.S. Navy were killed in action.

As we left Da Nang, I saw the roads were packed with Vietnamese. There were motor scooters and minibuses filled with sacks of rice, building materials, people, and animals. The buses looked like they would burst if one more thing was loaded in them. Women were walking on the side of the road with their ditty bop sticks over their shoulders, carrying a load on each end of the stick.

The further from Da Nang we drove, the less traffic there was on the road. The countryside was beautiful. Tropical trees, rice paddies, and water everywhere. There were Vietnamese farmers, mostly women, young kids, and old men working in the rice paddies along the way. The men and women had their black pajama pants rolled up to their knees, and they were wearing pointed bamboo hats. The children mostly wore short-sleeved shirts and short pants. None of them wore shoes, but most did wear hats. The women all chewed betel nut, and I could see the stains on what few teeth they had left. I heard they believed that chewing betel nut would make their breath smell good, decrease bad tempers, and make digesting food easier. To me, the only thing it appeared to do was turn their teeth black.

The country was nothing like what I had expected and nothing like the country I was used to back home. On the drive to the hill, I was in a state of shock. It had finally hit me square in the face. I was here, and I might not make it home alive. My senses had come alive. I could smell everything—the truck exhaust, the stagnant rice paddy water, the smoke from the hooches in the villages we passed, and my own fear, or maybe it was just sweat. In the bright sunlight I felt like I could see clearer than ever before. It was almost like I was looking through binoculars. Everything seemed so bright. But maybe it was just because there was no smog—there was no industry, just farming.

For the first in my life I felt naked without a rifle. All the marines we saw on patrol in the surrounding rice paddies or on bridge guard had M-16 rifles or M-79 grenade launchers. They wore flak jackets and helmets, and some wore 45-caliber pistols at their side. The driver and the marine riding shotgun were both armed, but none of us in the back had been issued a weapon yet. All I could think about was what I would do if we hit a mine or ran into an ambush. I would be here in the middle of Vietnam, not knowing where to run and not having a weapon. How would I protect myself? Little did I know at the time, this would become a recurring dream later in my life.

4. Hill 55

Soon Hill 55 loomed in the distance. It was a large hill dotted with green Marine Corps tents. There was concertina wire all around the outer perimeter of the hill, and fifty yards inside the wire was a trench with sandbag bunkers every few yards. The trench was chest deep and just wide enough to allow two people to pass. On the right side of the hill was a tall gun tower with a large ship's binoculars and a 50-caliber machine gun in the crow's nest. There was a massive gate where the road entered the hill, and I breathed a sigh of relief as we entered that gate. I was sure I would have a rifle before I left that gate again.

As long as I was in country, the enemy never launched a major assault on Hill 55. I discovered later, while talking to one of the local villagers, that when the French were stationed there the Viet Minh overran Hill 55. As the villager said, "The hill ran red with French blood," and ever since then they were very superstitious about the hill.

As soon as we passed through the gate, I noted there were three outdoor shops on the left. These shops were run by local Vietnamese. They sold clothing, candy, and cold soda, and marines could get a haircut there for a dollar. They had no electricity, so the Vietnamese barber would cut our hair with hand-operated clippers. Their main business was doing laundry for the marines on the hill. The first shop was operated by a Vietnamese lady named Swan, and it seemed to be the most popular one with the marines. There was always a crowd at Swan's, and she had the biggest supply of accessories for marines, but I think the thing that made it the most popular was that Swan was a very attractive young lady.

We wound around through the tents, past the mess tent and down the right side of the hill, past the 175s, and then came to a stop in front of a tent with a sign above the front door that read, "S-1." As we unloaded, a young corporal came out of the tent, had us line up, and collected our paperwork. He told us he would be getting us assigned to a unit within the regiment and for us to wait there, and then he disappeared back into the S-1 tent. There we were, ten frightened young men standing in the hot South Vietnamese sun with everything we owned in the duffel bags at our feet, not knowing what was going to happen next. As I looked around at the others standing there, I realized I did not know any of them. During the various stages of my training I had been separated from everyone I knew or had gone through boot camp with. I was arriving in Vietnam alone, not as part of a unit and without any buddies. For the first time in my life I felt very alone and realized that if I were to die here I would die alone. At that moment I had no idea how close I would become to some of the other scout snipers.

Did I mention we still did not have any rifles? I looked around the hillside. Among the tents were outhouses, two and three holers. Under each hole was half of a fifty-five-gallon drum with some diesel fuel in it. There was a hinged door on the back of the outhouses to access the drums. Every few days grunts from Headquarters Company would remove the drums, light the diesel fuel on fire to burn off the excrement, and then refuel and replace the drum.

Past the perimeter wire were more rice paddies and fields with tiny villages sprinkled here and there. In the distance to the west was a mountain range. I would later find out that it was called Charlie Ridge, and I would become very familiar with the area. Charlie Ridge was a haven for the Viet Cong and NVA. It provided safe cover and good access to supplies both from the Ho Chi Minh Trail and from the villagers in the delta. On the other side of Charlie Ridge from Hill 55 lay Laos and the Ho Chi Minh Trail.

When I examined the S-1 tent more closely, I noticed that under the S-1 sign was a sign that read, "Captain Porter, C.O." I wondered if this Captain Porter could be related to our neighbors back home, Mr. and Mrs. Porter. I knew they had an older son, who was in the Marine Corps, but Porter was a common name and the captain probably wasn't their son. Soon the corporal came back out and informed us we would have to spend the night on the hill until he could get us rides to our new units. Before he could return to the tent, I asked him if his Captain Porter was from New Mexico. He asked why I wanted to know, and I replied that our neighbors back home were named Porter.

The next thing I knew, I was standing in front of Captain Porter's desk. When I turned to face him sitting at his desk, I snapped to attention and saluted. He was indeed our neighbors' son, Captain Raymond Porter. I had seen Captain Porter once or twice years before, but each time he had been in civilian clothes. He looked a lot different sitting behind his desk in his uniform. He looked like a man who commanded authority. After exchanging introductions and some small talk, he offered me a job in his S-1 group, and I accepted. I was going to be an office pogue—I thought I just might get out of this conflict unscathed yet. That night I was taken to my tent and just two tents down was the 7th Marine Scout Sniper tent. In front of the tent was a big four-by-eight-foot signboard with the names of the snipers and the number of confirmed kills and probable kills each of them had. At that moment I knew I wanted my name on that board and I wanted it at the top.

The next morning I went to the armory tent and was issued an M-16 rifle and some magazines and ammo. All was finally right with the world.

Me on Hill 55 not long after arriving in country

Hill 55 looking out at Charlie Ridge photo courtesy of Victor Vilionis

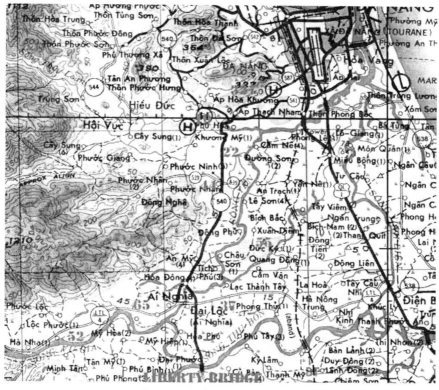

Map of 7th Marine Hills

The Secretary of the Navy takes pleasure in presenting the NAVY ACHIEVEMENT MEDAL to

LANCE CORPORAL JAY L. TAYLOR

UNITED STATES MARINE CORPS

for outstanding achievement in the superior performance of his duties in the field of professional achievement as set forth in the following

CITATION:

"While serving with the Seventh Marines, First Marine Division in connection with combat operations against the enemy in the Republic of Vietnam from 26 May 1968 to 4 June 1969, Lance Corporal Taylor performed his duties in an exemplary and highly professional manner. Initially assigned as a Casualty Clerk for the regiment, he displayed exceptional initiative and organizational ability while establishing a casualty clearance center at the logistical support activity located at Hill 55 during Operations Allen Brook and Mameluke Thrust which greatly expedited the forwarding of accurate casualty information to the division and parent commands. Fearlessly disregarding his own safety, he frequently traveled over roads made dangerous by hostile mines and, despite the hazards of enemy fire, visited every combat base within the Seventh Marines' Tactical Area of Responsibility in order to offer advice and guidance in the proper preparation of casualty reports. Having volunteered for a more active combat billet, he was reassigned as a Scout/Sniper with Headquarters Company in August 1968 and continued to distinguish himself by his outstanding performance of duty during numerous patrols through enemy controlled territory. Lance Corporal Taylor's professionalism, outstanding leadership and loyal devotion to duty contributed significantly to the accomplishment of his unit's mission and reflect great credit upon himself, the Marine Corps and the Naval Service."

The Combat Distinguishing Device is authorized.

FOR THE SECRETARY OF THE NAVY,

H. W. BUSE, JR.
LIEUTENANT GENERAL, U. S. MARINE CORPS
COMMANDING GENERAL, FLEET MARINE FORCE, PACIFIC

HEADQUARTERS
Seventh Marines
Fleet Marine Force, Pacific
FPO San Francisco 96602

1/PEP/ehd
1 Aug 1968

From: Adjutant, 7th Marine Regiment, Fleet Marine Force, Pacific, FPO San Francisco 96602
To: Commanding Officer, Headquarters Company, 7th Marine Regiment, FPO San Francisco 96602

Subj: Letter of Continuity, case of Lance Corporal Jay L. TAYLOR 240 44 66/0311/8541 USMC

Ref: (a) 1st Marine Division Order 1650.1A

1. In accordance with the provisions of reference (a), the following information concerning the performance of the subject Marine while assigned to my section is provided for continuity purposes in considering him for an appropriate meritorious service award.

    a. Lance Corporal TAYLOR served as the Regimental Casualty Clerk during the period 5 May to 23 July 1968. In this capacity he repeatedly exercised excellent judgement and initiative in processing casualty reports. His recommendations for improving reporting procedures have resulted in reducing processing time for casualty reports by 1/3 and have simplified the system utilized by units in the field to the point that casualties can be reported in less than 1/2 the time previously required.

    b. During operations, Allen Brook and Mameluke Thrust, Lance Corporal TAYLOR established a casualty clearing center at the LSA and operated it for 47 days without one error.

    c. In an attempt to insure that all units were thoroughly aware of proper procedures to be utilized in casualty reporting, he repeatedly made trips over hazardous roads, subjected to sniper fire and mines, to every company within the TAOR to give classes or render any assistance as may be needed.

2. Throughout his service within the adjutant's section, Lance Corporal TAYLOR has displayed a keen interest in his job and the mission of his unit. I consider his service to warrant recognition by an appropriate meritorious service award.

R. E. PORTER
Captain USMC

5. My Tenure as an S-1 Office Pogue

One of my instructors had said that it took nine people in the rear to support every one grunt in combat. We had to acquire food, water, mail, clothing, weapons, and ammo, all of which had to be delivered to the base camps and to the bush by land, sea, and air. We also needed medical care, communication support, road builders, bridge builders, intelligence gathering, and all kinds of other logistical support. There were truck drivers, pilots, mechanics, doctors, nurses, cooks, clerks, and morticians. All of these people were in Vietnam, away from their families, and they were exposed to many of the same daily hazards and had to endure the same heat, bugs, snakes, rats, mosquitoes, and mortar attacks as the soldiers in the bush. Many of the names of the people who served in the rear now appear on the Wall. Their jobs required a special type of courage which, as I was about to find out, I did not possess. For all of these unsung heroes, I say, "Thank you."

Captain Porter noticed in my paperwork that I had taken a typing class in high school. (The only reason I had taken typing was because I thought it would be an easy class and provide a good chance to meet some girls.) The recruiter had given me a typing test when I joined the Marine Corps, and I had scored fifteen words per minute with mistakes. That was about to change.

My job as an S-1 clerk consisted of three main tasks. First, I was in charge of all R&R allocations for the regiment. This made me very popular with the marines wanting to go to Hawaii. It was a hard spot to get and was usually reserved for married marines and officers. Second, I was responsible for allocating all new recruits assigned to 7th Marine Regiment to the three battalions in the regiment. I would also allocate out promotions that were issued to the regiment. My third and biggest job was that I was the new 7th Marine Regimental casualty clerk. This would become my most time-consuming job and the job I dreaded the most.

After a marine had been in country for six or seven months he was eligible for an out-of-country R&R. R&R stood for Rest and Relaxation, but some called it Rape and Revenge. This was a one-week leave to places like Hawaii, Japan, Taiwan, Sydney, or Okinawa. Each marine was required to submit a request form indicating his first three choices for R&R. Each month the 1st Marine Division would allocate a number of openings for each of these locations to the 7th Marine Regiment. My job was to sort through the request forms and give as many marines as possible their first choice, and those that did not get their first choice got their second or third choice. Very seldom were there more requests than allocations. When there were, the unlucky ones were placed at the top of the list for the next month. This part of my job was not very difficult and did not take up much of my time.

New guys in country were not very difficult to process either. The battalions always needed all of the new recruits they could get. I just divided them up as evenly as possible unless one battalion had taken heavy causalities for the month, in which case they received more. Promotions were the same. I divided them evenly between the battalions, and a few were allocated to regimental HQ. I worked closely with the battalion clerks to try to fill their needs.

As the casualty clerk I was responsible for reporting all casualties to Regimental Colonel Robert L. Nichols twice daily, at 8 AM and 8 PM. I was required to give him a complete list of all 7th Marine Regimental Marines who had been killed or wounded during that twelve-hour time period. If they had been wounded I had to report what type of wound they had sustained and to what location they had been medevaced. My reports listed their last name, the last four digits of their service number, and which unit they were with. This was in the days before computers. All of the files were hard files, and all research had to be done by hand. All reports were typed on manual typewriters using carbon paper. This job took up most of my time. I had standing orders to notify the colonel anytime day or night if two specific people in the regiment were hit. One was Captain Charles

Rob, commanding officer of Lima Company and the president's son-in-law, and the other was a senator's son.

Often I would be up all night long, on the radio, getting casualty information from the troops in the field. I hated forcing them to strike a match at night so they get the last four numbers off the dog tags of their fellow marines who had been killed in action. Many times I could hear the sound of gunfire and artillery rounds exploding in the background. I could hear the frustration in their voices as they struggled to get the information I needed, but those amazing grunts always managed to get whatever info I needed. The colonel always got his report on time.

The part of the job I dreaded the most, even though this was only necessary a few times, were the times that I was required go up on top of the hill where the helipad was located and open body bags in order to get the serial numbers from the dog tags of the dead so I could properly identify them. These calls were usually at night when a chopper carrying dead marines bound for Da Nang would stop at Hill 55 so the bodies could be identified. I think I could have gotten used to working with dead bodies, but this was different. With my flashlight in hand I would go to each body bag, unzip it, and search for the dog tags in order to record the service numbers. Since the dog tags were normally worn around the neck, I was required to shine my flashlight into the face of each of these dead marines, sometimes as many as six or eight of them, while I searched for their tags. Some appeared very peaceful and others were disfigured as a result of their wounds. As much as I have tried over the years, I have never completely forgotten the looks on their faces and their mangled bodies. These were American marines who had been killed in action. These men had earned an honor and place of reverence where none of us belonged. They had earned their privacy and their peace. I always felt like I was violating this when I was performing this duty. These were the ones who had paid the ultimate price, and I did not deserve to walk among them. It was an incredibly solemn and saddening feeling that totally consumed me each time I had to perform this task. I have never forgotten that feeling.

6. Cpl Gang

Cpl Gang bunked in the same tent I was in. He worked in Phy-Ops, (Physiological Operations). He was part of a team that included Sergeant Fong, a Kit Carson Scout, and an army officer. Their job was to travel throughout our TOAR and broadcast propaganda to the enemy in an attempt to persuade them to surrender. They broadcast mainly at night. The army officer had a permanent duty station in Da Nang, and he seldom visited Hill 55 or worked with the team. The army furnished the team a truck and all the broadcasting equipment, allowing Gang full-time use of the truck.

On one occasion my folks sent me some pinion nuts and I decided to see if I could mess with Sgt Fong a little. I knew he was in our office tent one afternoon, so I walked in eating some of the pinion nuts. I was sure he would have no idea what they were. There were old wooden desks on each side of the tent and one at the end. Each desk had an old type writer on it, and behind each desk was an assortment of old filing cabinets which contained data about the 7th Marine Regiment. Sgt Fong was in his late thirties or early forties, five foot four inches tall, of average build and clean shaven, and he always wore a clean, pressed South Vietnam uniform. He and Gang were standing at the end desk talking to one of the other clerks when I walked in. I walked right up to Sgt. Fong and held a handful of pinions out and asked him if he wanted some.

He looked at them, and as he grabbed a handful he said to me, "Ahhhh, pinion seeds … Where you from, Texas?" I couldn't believe it. He had never been out of Vietnam, and he knew what pinion nuts were. He even knew what region of the States they came from. He never would tell me who, but someone from Texas must have offered him some pinions before. He had been around since the time the

French were in Vietnam and there probably wasn't much he hadn't seen.

Cpl Gang was from New Jersey. He was three or four inches taller than I was and outweighed me by forty pounds. Shortly after we met he let me know that he had been a state champion in judo or one of those beat-the-crap-out-of-you martial arts. This should have been my first clue not to mess with him. Most of the other guys in the tent did not seem to care much for Gang, but he and I got along pretty well. Since Gang had the use of the army truck, he had access to Da Nang almost anytime he wanted to go, and consequently he had access to the girls of the night and the hard liquor available there.

This was where the problems started. Every time Gang came back from Da Nang with a load of whiskey, he thought he and I needed to drink all of it, and every time he got drunk he wanted to wrestle. As I mentioned earlier, I had wrestled in high school. I was even pretty good at it. I had placed in the state tournament. So the first time he wanted to wrestle I was game for it. Well, let me tell you it didn't take me long to figure out that I was no match for Gang. Even when he was drunk he could bounce me off the plywood floor and sidewalls of our tent like I was a tennis ball. Maybe that was the reason no one else seemed to care much for him. Gang was a great guy, but I sure never missed those wrestling matches.

After a couple of months, I had traveled to all of the regimental battalion headquarters and many company headquarters and worked with their clerks on ways we could make the casualty reporting more efficient for all of us and thus help to cut down on the workload for all of us.

After I had been working in the S-1 office for nearly three months, the time came for Captain Porter to rotate back to the states, and I knew I did not want to do this job any longer. I truly felt that I would rather risk being one of those individuals in the body bags than continue being the casualty clerk, so I asked the captain for a transfer. This was hard to do because I felt a loyalty to the captain. I knew he had been trying to keep me alive when he first offered me the job in S-1. I let him know that I appreciated what he had done for me but that I was unhappy in my current job and I would like to be transferred out. I told him I would like to get into the sniper platoon, but if that was not possible I would rather be in one of the grunt companies than to continue working as the casualty clerk. For the second time in less than three months, Captain Porter probably saved my life. He had me transferred to the sniper platoon.

By this time, I could type one hundred words a minute with very few mistakes, but I had only shot my rifle a few times at rocks off the side of the hill. My world was about to change again.

June 5, 1968, Robert F. Kennedy was shot and mortally wounded in Los Angeles just after winning the California Democratic presidential primary election. Nearly four months later I turned nineteen years old.

7. Scout Sniper Platoon

Snipers and scouts have been used in warfare since the beginning of time. Normally they were disbanded and not kept as part of the peace-time military. Vietnam and the role Scout Snipers played there changed that forever.

The Vietnam-era sniper organization was started in Vietnam in 1965. One group that was instrumental in the beginning was, Major Robert "Bob" Russell and five others; MGySgt George Hurt, GySgt Marvin Lange, MSgt Donald Barker, Sgt Jim Bowen, and Sgt Bob Goller. There were others in Vietnam during that same time period and over the next few years who also made significant contributions to the Scout Sniper program. There is a more detailed account of the Vietnam-era sniper program beginnings in the book *Inside the Crosshairs, Snipers in Vietnam* by Michael Lee Lanning. I have met Major Russell, who is now retired and living in Arizona. He is a real gentleman and a true marine.

Snipers in 7th Marine Regiment were assigned to two-man teams—a spotter and a shooter—and they normally stayed together until one of the pair rotated home or was wounded or killed. Others, like myself, worked with many different partners during our tour in Nam. It did not take long to form a very close bond with or a strong dislike for your partner. We were very dependent on each other. When we were out in the bush, we had to be very aware of where the other was at all times in case of an attack. Since I was the team leader and carried the 700, my partner carrier the automatic weapon and was my protector in case of a firefight. As a spotter he was invaluable. He helped estimate range. Many times he spotted the enemy first and spotted the impact of my round so I could adjust my hold off. The term "hold off" referred to how far we had to hold the center of the crosshairs over or under the target in order to hit it, based on the difference between the distance to the target and the point of aim point of impact of the rifle. I never wanted my partner out of my sight without me knowing where he was. In return I never stepped out of his sight without telling him where I was going. I would even tell my partner if I was going to step into the brush to relieve myself. This became a habit that to this day I still have not completely broken. At times I still catch myself telling a friend I am with that I am just going to the bathroom and will be right back. Then I realize I gave him more information than he really needed to know.

There were not many snipers present the morning I arrived at the sniper tent. Standing at the top of the wooden steps leading up to the tent door was Sergeant Mark Webb.

"What do you want?" were his first words to me. Sgt Webb had been in country for two years at the time, and he didn't have much use for new guys. My first impression was that he was a real hard ass. I found out later that Mark was really a very compassionate person.

"My name is Taylor and I just got transferred here from S-1," I said.

"Well, grab your gear and you can pick out a bunk," he replied.

Inside the tent were cots lining opposite walls with a narrow walkway down the middle. To the right side of the door was a large pile of duffel bags and gear. On one of the cots was a 50-cal machine gun. Rumor had it that a couple of the snipers had borrowed it from the 1st Marine Division Band in Da Nang. I never could figure out why the division band would need to have a 50-cal machine gun. Maybe that is why no one ever returned it. There was a door at the back of the tent, and there were a couple of shotguns leaning against the back wall. The shotguns were sometimes used by nighttime killer teams. Some of the cots had gear under them and some did not. I stored my gear under one of the empty cots. This would be my main base camp for the next ten months. I spent the rest of the day moving my gear in and becoming acquainted with all of the weapons in the tent. By day's end I had met all of the snipers who were on the hill besides Sergeant Webb.

There was Sergeant Ross, a large barrel-chested individual who was very intimidating especially when he had been drinking. Sergeant Hada, a short oriental guy who everyone said was crazy,

Sergeant Martinez, Corporal Hanna, and Corporal Poole. All of these guys had been in Nam at least one tour, and most had extended one or more times. Some were on their second or third extensions. A tour was thirteen months, and then you could extent in Nam for six more months with a thirty-day leave in between. The other snipers in the platoon were out working with various companies in the regiment. Our CO was Captain Head. He was the CO of headquarters company, and he had very little to do with the daily operations of the sniper platoon.

I stayed on the hill for the next few days waiting to get assigned to a team leader. Daily I would go to the perimeter of the hill and target practice with one of the 700s. Twice I went to the gun tower with some of the other snipers. We had a 50-cal mounted on a tripod up in the crow's nest of the tower. There was a twelve-power Unertl scope mounted on the 50. I did get a chance to shoot at a couple of VC with it. They were probably over 2,500 yards away. I didn't hit either of them, but I scared the hell out of both of them. They sure could run fast. After a week, I finally went out for the first time.

Sgt Webb must have drawn the short straw because he had to take myself and another new guy, LCpl Escudero, out for the first time. We caught a ride to Hill 22 and were first assigned to 3rd Battalion. The 7th Marine Regiment had units stationed on Hills 65, 52, 42, 37, 25, 22, and 10. Units were often moved from one hill to another in support of major operations and in response to increased enemy activity. As attachments to the various units, the snipers were afforded a chance to work in all of these areas.

Sergeant Webb was a big man and three years older than me, but at the time it seemed like he was twenty years older than me. He had been in Nam for one tour and one extension already, and his name was near the top of the board of confirmed kills. I know he was not pleased to have to take two green snipers to the bush for their first time. Lance Corporal Escudero had been in the Corps longer than I had, but he was new in country, so I felt I had more experience than him even though I had been in an office for the last three months. Escudero had been on sea duty as a guard on a naval ship before being transferred to Nam. He was still very much "Marine Corps spit and polish" and did not seem to fit in with the rest of the snipers very well.

Our first time out with India Company was an uneventful one but very interesting, for me at least. Everything was new, exciting, and a little bit scary. We patrolled across large rice paddies, on top of the dykes dividing the paddies. When we left the rice paddies we traveled through tall grass and jungle-type vegetation, staying on a footpath that wound through the jungle until we came to a large clearing with a number of grass hooches. It was a very eerie feeling to walk through the village and see the people standing there staring at us as we passed by. I could smell tea cooking over the small fires in the hooches and I noticed there were dried, paper-thin sheets of rice on the hooch roofs. The Vietnamese would make a paste out of rice and roll it into very large paper-thin, tortilla-like sheets and place them on the roofs of their hooches to dry. The Vietnamese women would break off a piece of these rice sheets and rehydrate them in water. Then they would cut them into thin slices to make their noodles. Their main diet consisted of rice, rice noodles, and vegetables. Fish and some meat were also used in their cooking, but the villages had no means of refrigeration and I never saw any of the villagers butcher one of their cows, so I never asked where the meat came from. The villages did not have power, running water, or outhouses—they just went to the bathroom out behind their hooch. Toilet paper was a luxury they did not have. The pajama-style pants the women wore were baggy in the legs so when they had to urinate they would just roll up a pant leg, squat down, and go. Their idea of modesty was very different than ours.

I saw my first dung beetle rolling a dung ball along the ground. This mission was also the first time I ever saw a Vietnamese Pot-bellied Pig. They ran loose in the villages. At first I thought there was something wrong with them, like maybe they had a bellyful of worms. The Vietnamese Pot-bellied Pig was actually a breed of pig that originated in Vietnam. Their ears stood straight up, they were sway backed, and their bellies nearly dragged on the ground. The large ones appeared to weigh over two hundred pounds. These pigs were so ugly; the idea of eating their meat was not a pleasant thought.

Webb kept a very watchful eye on us as we traveled through the countryside and villages. The squad we were with had to sweep through one of the villages and search for weapons and food stashes. During this sweep, and in spite of Webb's watchful eye, Escudero and I managed to get separated from Sergeant Webb and the rest of the squad. I knew where we were supposed to meet up with the rest of the platoon, so Escudero and I headed that way. We arrived there long before Webb and the squad. When Webb arrived later, he was really pissed off at us. Webb and the squad had torn the village apart looking for us, and Webb had managed to step on a booby trap. The only thing that saved him was that the plunger on top of the bomb he stepped on had bent instead of pushing down and detonating the charge. He must have chewed our asses out for an hour. I made sure that I never got separated from my partner again.

8. First Kill

During the first few weeks I was partnered up with Sgt Webb he had taken a couple of shots at a few VC we had spotted while we were out on patrol. I spotted for him, and I know he hit at least one of them. We were all very good shots, but we all missed our fair share of the time. The best chance we normally had of hitting the enemy was when he was stopped and presented a still target. After the first shot we would be shooting at moving targets, which are very difficult to hit at long range. They never seemed to run directly away from us, which would have made them slightly easier targets. A man weaving in and out of the brush at 700 yards is a very difficult target to hit—I don't care how good of a shot you think you are.

One day while on patrol with a squad from Charlie Company in the foothills near Charlie Ridge, Webb and I separated from the squad to find a hide from where we could watch the adjacent ridge. We planned to stay there until later in the day when the squad came back to pick us up. We had been in our hide for an hour when Webb spotted some VC on the ridge across from us, 650 yards out. He handed the 700 to me and said, "Here, you take this one." I was surprised. I had not expected this. I had not been in the field very long, and to get a chance to take my first shot at the enemy with the 700 this soon was not the norm.

I wanted my first kill, or at least I thought I did. The desire to get my first kill had started from the minute I volunteered for the snipers and the desire had steadily grown stronger. All of my training and mental conditioning, or brainwashing, was in preparation for this. From the first day I had seen the sign in front of the sniper tent with the kill tally on it, my desire to get my first kill had intensified. I could tell from being around the other snipers in the platoon who had kills that it was a private club and there was only one way in. Place the crosshairs of a nine-power scope on a man, squeeze the trigger, and know your bullet was the one that killed him.

I quickly got into position and located the VC in the rifle scope. At least ten of them were walking up the ridge in single file, coming in and out of view as they weaved through the thick vegetation. Due to the thick vegetation there was only one spot at the crest of the ridge where when they passed through it I could get a clean shot. They were visible from the waist up for only a brief moment. As I watched, I couldn't believe my luck. The column stopped and one of them was standing right in the opening.

Webb was watching through the binoculars and whispered, "Hold a little high. They are at least 700 yards out." There was no wind. I put the crosshairs on the man's head and then raised the center of the crosshairs a foot and a half above his head and squeezed the trigger. I was trying for a body shot. I was not prepared for what happened next—I had thought I was but I wasn't. I was in a good prone shooting position, so the recoil of the rifle did not knock me off of the sight picture. My shot was high, or he was closer than the 700 yards we had estimated and I watched as the bullet struck his head. At that distance with a nine-power scope I could see the impact of the bullet—his head distorted out of shape and snapped sideways as if something was trying to rip it off his shoulders, and he dropped out of sight instantly. It was like slow motion and yet it happened in the blink of an eye. That picture is as clear in my mind today as it was forty years ago. Webb said, "You nailed the bastard." Instinctively I was immediately searching for another shot at one of his comrades, but they were all down and out of sight. Sgt. Webb also glassed for another opportunity but there were none. The body was hidden from our view by the brush, so even if we could get the platoon commander to our position we would not be able to get a confirmed kill without being able to see the body, and there was no way we were going to attempt to reach the kill site from where we were. After a few more minutes of glassing, Sgt Webb said, "Let's get the hell out of here in case they come after us," so we left and saw no more action the rest of the day.

The weight of what I had just done hit me like a ton of bricks. It was a tremendous letdown—I didn't feel the joy or pride I had thought I would at killing my first man. At the same time I felt very little remorse about what I had just done. However, I did realize I had just broken the worst taboo possible—"Thou shalt not kill." How would I be able to justify what I had done when my time came? I had just killed a man who was merely standing there waiting for the man in front of him to move. I knew then I could never go back—I could never bring the man I had just killed back to life. I had not yet managed to completely dehumanize these people, and for that reason alone I had mixed feelings about what I had done. It would take a while longer before I no longer looked at these people as humans, and could justify what I was doing by rationalizing that each time I killed one of them, I might be saving one of our lives.

"What greater sin, can one man inflict on another, than the taking of his life, and how will I be judged when my time comes?"

Most of the Vietnam veterans who returned home brought their demons home with them, and in spite of the fact that often their homecoming was not a pleasant one; they managed to fit back into society. "85 percent of Vietnam veterans made a successful transition to civilian life. Vietnam veterans' personal income exceeds that of our non-veteran age group by more than 18 percent. Vietnam veterans have a lower unemployment rate than our non-vet age group. 87 percent of the American people hold Vietnam vets in high esteem."[1]

---

[1] From a speech given by Lieutenant General Barry R. McCaffrey, assistant to the Chairman of the Joint Chiefs of Staff, to Vietnam veterans and visitors gathered at The Wall on Memorial Day, 1993.

9. Bagging the Bush

We worked with various units based on hills throughout the 7th Marine Regiment TAOR. When we were not on patrol with one of the squads, we rested up on the company hill and stood tower watch. We were usually out for one or two days at a time, longer if we were on an operation. During the day we would go with one of the squads on patrol, drop off somewhere along the patrol route, find a position where we had a good vantage, and conceal ourselves for most of the day trying to catch the VC or NVA moving around so we could get a shot. Before dark we would leave our hide and meet back up with the platoon or they would circle back and pick us up.

We were supplied with C-rations for our meals when we were out in the bush. C-rations came in cardboard boxes, one meal per box and twelve meals per case. A one-day supply of C-rations was designed around a 3,800-calorie-a-day diet. Each meal contained a main course packed in a tin can. Some of the main dishes were cooked meat, cooked pork, turkey slices, scrambled eggs, and the always-popular ham and lima beans to mention a few. The ration boxes also contained a canned dessert, a can of fruit, toilet paper, a small pack of cigarettes; heat tablets to use for cooking, instant coffee, and a P-38 can opener. The fruit came in tall cans, and the main three were peaches, apricots, and fruit cocktail. I always saved the empty peach cans to make coffee in. The coffee would take on the flavor of whatever had been in the can, and apricot-flavored coffee was not very desirable to say the least.

There were also Halazone tablets to use for purifying water in case we had to fill our canteens in the field. If you were lucky enough to have a bottle of Tabasco sauce with you, you were considered a gourmet cook. There were occasions when we were given Long Range Patrol Rations, or Lurps, as they were called. Lurps were developed in 1964, and they were much lighter than C-rations. Lurps were a freeze-dried meal in a vacuum-packed plastic pouch. Like C-rations, they came with a plastic spoon and a brown-foil accessory packet containing coffee, cream substitute, sugar, salt, candy-coated gum (two pieces), toilet paper, a book of matches, and a pack of four cigarettes.

When we were out for more than a daytime patrol, the company headquarters radioed in the patrol routes for the night. Each squad had a different patrol route, and we would go with one of the squads. The patrol routes usually consisted of approximately eight checkpoints. The squad leader would mark the checkpoints on his map, and when it got dark we would walk to each checkpoint and the radio man would call in our position when we arrived at each checkpoint. This would normally take all night. This type of patrolling resulted in very little sleep for the grunts, and it could go on for days at a time before the unit returned to the base camp for some rest.

One night soon after we had started on a patrol, the squad leader stopped and asked Sgt Webb if he would mind if they bagged the bush for the night. The patrol routes were normally a big circle which brought you back close to where it started. When a squad bagged the bush they would only make one or two checkpoints and then they would stop and sleep while each squad member took his turn standing watch and calling in when they should have arrived at the next checkpoint. At daybreak they would precede to the last checkpoint just as if they had been on patrol all night.

Sgt Webb told the squad leader he did not care and that the three of us snipers would take our turn at watch also. We stopped at a village that was located inside an old ARVN (Army of the Republic of Vietnam) compound. We camped for the night beside an old, abandoned hooch. Across from us was an old Vietnamese Army hospital which was still in partial use by the local villagers. The exterior walls of the hospital were the adobe type and the roof was made of grass. It was decided the three of us snipers would stand the last three watches—that way we would not have to call in any checkpoints.

We settled in and tried to get what sleep we could while the grunts took turns standing watch. Webb was the first one of us to be woken up to stand watch, and then he woke me for my turn. After my time was up I woke Escudero for his turn and then settled back down and tried to get some more sleep as the first streaks of light were just starting to show in the sky.

Before I could get back to sleep, I heard Escudero saying very softly, "Halt! Who goes there?" I thought I was dreaming. Again I heard, "Halt! Who goes there?" This was something I would expect to hear when I was in boot camp, not in the predawn hours in Nam. I opened my eyes and saw Escudero had his rifle pointed at on old Vietnamese man taking a leak by the corner of the hospital. Again he called out, "Halt! Who goes there?" Luckily I stopped him before he shot the poor old guy. When I finished letting him know how stupid his actions were and how if it really had been a VC he would have gotten himself killed, it was time to wake up Webb and the rest of the squad. Of course I had to tell them what had happened and we all had a good laugh at Escudero's expense. I never did care much for Escudero and I am sure the feeling was mutual. Escudero did not make it as a sniper. A few weeks later he was washed out of the sniper platoon and transferred to a grunt company.

10. The Gang

After being partnered up with Webb for a few weeks, I had met most of the other snipers in the platoon. We usually ran into other snipers on the trips we made back to Hill 55 to get paid, pick up mail, or get reassigned. Normally we would spend a night or two on Hill 55 before going back out to our assigned company. They were a great bunch of guys.

LCpl Robinson was very quiet and good natured. Robbie, as we called him, was a tall, blond eighteen-year-old young man. He had a large nose, and we all teased him about it. We nicknamed him "The Beak." It never seemed to bother him much or he just never let it show, which was good for him, because if he had we would have only teased him more. I really liked Robbie and always hoped we would be partnered up, but we never were. LCpl Timothy Pearson was Robbie's partner for a long time. Once when Robbie and I were both stationed on Hill 10 and firing at some VC from the tower, I touched a round off, not realizing how close the barrel of my rifle was to Robbie's ear. The percussion from the muzzle blast nearly left him deaf in his left ear.

LCpl Colin McGee was from Michigan. He had a loud voice and was a funny guy to be around. He had an infectious laugh. I really liked McGee, and being around him always seemed to cheer me up. Foster and McGee were partners.

Corporal Foster had been a grunt for his first tour in Nam. Foster was a private person, and even though he had a smile on his face much of the time he seemed to be very solemn. A tour with the grunts could really affect a man. At times Foster would sit in his chair with a blank look on his face. It was a look we called the "thousand-yard stare." Many young marines who had seen more death and human suffering than any person should ever witness developed this stare.

LCpl Claude Alfred "Stony" was from Texas, and I thought he was a quiet guy until I went on R&R with him. We went to Australia together and had adjoining rooms in a hotel. We had a great time and managed to stay drunk almost around the clock while we were there. Stony was a real chick magnet.

LCpl Ray Gonzales "Gunny" was also from Texas, and he had extended in Vietnam to keep his brother from having to go. When he was out of the bush he always wore a pair of dark sunglasses. Gunny and J.D. Butler were partners.

LCpl William "Bill" Martin and Stony were partners, and maybe that is why I thought Stony was kind of a quiet person. Bill was like a fart in a whirlwind. He was going all of the time. I am not sure how he managed to sit still long enough to function as a sniper, but he and Stony were a very successful team. One time while on Hill 55 Bill tricked me into taking a long pull off of a jug of moonshine that Chuck Butler's mother had sent him from Alabama. She had put the shine in a soap bottle she had attempted to clean, but it still retained the soapy taste. To this day, I have never tasted anything worse than moonshine mixed with dish soap.

LCpl Gomez, "Big G", was another person I couldn't help but like. I used to call him, "Big G Little Oooo Gomez." He was the type of person that you couldn't make mad. He always had a smile on his face. Gomez was a short man and just about as big around as he was tall. He reminded me of a little teddy bear. Big G and Chuck Butler were partners. When Gomez came back from his thirty-day leave on his last six-month extension in Nam, he did not return to the sniper platoon. He served as a door gunner in a chopper for his last six months in country.

LCpl Charles "Chuck" Butler was a very easy-going and likeable person. If he ever got mad about anything I was never aware of it. Chuck lost two partners while he was in Vietnam and it would change his life forever.

LCpl John Perry and I were partners for a while soon after he arrived in the platoon. John had been in a grunt company before coming to the snipers. I liked John; he was a very confident person. He had also learned a lot during his time as a grunt and it made him a very valuable partner. John had a sense of humor, but most of the time he was very businesslike. It did not take long in a grunt company to rob a young man of his innocence.

Cpl Rick Rush was very likeable and easy going. I am not sure why Rush stayed in Nam so long—he had the kind of personally that would have allowed him to fit in with the hippy movement just as well. Rush was our resident flower child who carried a Remington 700 instead of flowers.

Some of the others were: LCpl J.D. Butler, LCpl Bridges, Cpl King, LCpl Jepsen, and LCpl Tim Pearson. We normally had twenty to twenty-two snipers in the platoon who were deployed to various units in the regiment. We never called each other by our first names; it was either our last name or a nickname. Because we were out with different units most of the time, I never had a chance to get to know many of the guys very well. There were also some in our platoon I never had the opportunity to meet. They were either wounded and shipped out of country or killed before I had a chance to meet them.

11. William L. Mott

After I had worked with Webb for a few weeks, he felt I was ready for a permanent partner and I was assigned to Cpl Poole as his spotter. Poole was about five foot seven and had a muscular build. When I joined him, Poole had less than two months left in country. We were sent to Hill 37 to work with Charlie 1/7. For living quarters, we were assigned to a small, rat-infested bunker located next to the tower. It was just big enough for two cots. The dog handlers had the hooch next to us, and they kept their two dogs tied up outside our hooch.

I don't know what kind of a sniper Poole had been before I was partnered up with him, but for the month we were partners he was definitely part of the reason snipers had a bad reputation with some units. During the month we were on Hill 37, we only went out three times, and we did not get any kills.

Every morning Poole would go to the command bunker for the morning briefing and to see if there were any patrols we could go out with. Each morning he would return with excuses as to why none of the patrols were right for us, and then, all day long, Poole would pace the floor in our bunker and look at himself in the little mirror that was hanging on the end wall. He must have been proud of his looks because each time he looked at his image in the mirror, he would slap each side of his face like he was trying to make his cheeks red. Not only was it boring to sit on the hill for a month and do nothing, I was beginning to feel ashamed to be a sniper. I pressured Poole as much as I could to get us out in the field more, but it was to no avail. Maybe it was just because he was short (short was what we called someone who did not have much time left in country) and he did not want to go out and risk being hit. I didn't care. I was getting bored sitting on the hill and had grown to dislike Poole.

After a month we returned to Hill 55 to get paid. I had had all I could stand of Poole's pacing and patting his face as he stared in that mirror, so I told the platoon sergeant I would not work with Poole any longer. I explained my reasons to him and asked him if I could be assigned to another team leader. I knew this could get me in trouble because Poole was the team leader, he had much more time in country, and he outranked me. I must have not been the only one who knew what Poole was like, because the next day, I was informed I would be a new team leader. I was given my own 700 and a new partner. His name was William L. Mott.

Mott was a big kid from Tennessee, and he had a thick southern accent. We hit it off right away. My mom was born and raised on the Alabama / Tennessee state line and as far as Mott was concerned that made us kin. We became very close. He immediately nicknamed me Jason. When Mott first arrived on Hill 55, one of the guys there tagged him with the nickname "Zeno." We shared stories with each other about our families, what our parents were like, the good times we had had with our friends, and of course our girlfriends. We learned a lot about each other and our families back home. These stories were our only link to the "real world," as we called it. It was important for us to remember there was another world other than the screwed up one we were in.

We shared our pictures and our letters with each other when we got them. I knew Mott's dad was a part-time preacher and a part-time drinker. Mott talked a lot about his mother and the rest of his family. It sounded like he was very close to them. I think he felt joining the Marine Corps and sending money back home was the best way he could help them. Mott and I even agreed to contact each other's family if either one of us ever got hit. It was a promise that would take me many years to fulfill.

When Mott found out I chewed tobacco, he had his family send him a package of King Bee Twist chewing tobacco from home. When it arrived he handed the package to me and said, "Here, Jason, try some." He then watched wide-eyed as I opened the package, tore off a plug, and started chewing it. He looked like a big kid watching me open a Christmas present. "How is it?" he asked. It was terrible, but I didn't have the heart to tell him. Over the next few days I chewed all of it and never let him know how bad I really thought it was. It would have broken his heart, to think I didn't like his favorite brand of chewing tobacco, his parents had sent him from back home in Tennessee.

We worked with different companies from the Hill 22 area and managed to get a few kills along the way. I was the team leader and carried the 700, and Mott was my spotter. I would let him carry the 700 once in a while, and he did get a chance to take a couple shots. He was like a kid with a new bike when I let him carry the sniper rifle. When we weren't in the field, I kept the 700 in its case. Mott wrote, "Jason and Zeno" on the case, and he carried it every time we traveled to Hill 55 and back. He was very proud to be a sniper.

We went out on four-man killer teams at night a few times but seldom had much success. At night the mosquitoes were so big and numerous they could carry a man off. We could not use any kind of bug dope for fear Charlie might smell it. We had to sit there all night and let the mosquitoes feast on us.

Killing was becoming easier. The more I killed, the less I thought about it. Seeing other marines getting killed and mangled made the killing easier to accept. We made friends with the grunts in the different units with which we worked, and it was always painful when one of them got wounded or worse yet, killed. I only ever saw three grunts serve their full thirteen months in the bush with a grunt company and rotate home. Most of them were wounded, killed, or transferred out of the field before their time in country was up. I had the utmost respect for those marines. They were the workhorses of the Marine Corps, and seldom did they get the credit they so justly deserved.

September 20, 1968, I completed another Scout Sniper school. This one was in Da Nang. It was seven days before my nineteenth birthday. The School lasted only five days. LCpl Gonzales and I attended it. It really wasn't as much a school, as it was a chance to sight our rifles in at known ranges. We did get to sit in on one interesting class. During the class, we were given a briefing on some classified explosive ordinances being used along the Ho Chi Minh Trail. I never saw one other than in that classroom.

Any time Mott and I had to return to Hill 55 from one of the regimental hills, we had to pass by the 1st Division HQ outside of

Da Nang. If we had the time we would stop by Freedom Hill PX and do some shopping. If we could, we would get someone from one of the other branches of the service to use our ration card, and buy a jug of whiskey for us. Enlisted marines ranked E-5 and under were not allowed to buy hard liquor. Also, there was a movie theater, and we would stop and see a movie if we had the time.

There was an area just outside of Da Nang called Dog Patch. It was the red light district. There were numerous little shacks alongside the road that housed call girls. Occasionally some of the marines we were traveling with would want to stop at Dog Patch to visit one of the girls. When they did, I always stayed outside and watched for the MPs. I had no desire to visit the call girls, and not because of any moral issues I might have had. There was the concern of venereal disease, but mainly I thought sleeping with one of these young Vietnamese girls would have somehow made them more human to me. I did not want that to happen. Usually one of the mama sans would stand outside with me and try to talk me into going inside. On one occasion, while I was waiting outside, a mama san tried to get me to go inside with her. I kept declining until finally she said to me, "Ahhh, you must be a cherry boy ... I souvenir you boom-boom free." I laughed and politely declined.

While Mott and I were partners and were deployed to Hill 22, I got deathly ill. I had a roaring case of diarrhea, and the corpsman had nothing that would even slow it down. After a week of trying the corpsman finally sent me to the 1st Marine Division hospital in Da Nang. After seeing the doctor, he gave me some medicine, and sent me to get some X-rays. The X-ray machine was located next to the helicopter landing pad in a large airplane hangar where incoming wounded were treated. Choppers would land on the asphalt pad next to the hangar and then rush the wounded into the hangar, where teams of doctors and nurses would work on them. As I was standing in line to get x-rayed, I watched as they brought in a wounded Korean marine. He was placed on the table next to me, and a group of doctors and nurses ran over and started working on him. None of them could read Korean, so they were unable to read his medevac card that had been filled out in the field by the corpsman. His heart had quit beating, so they brought out the defibrillator and began their attempts to resuscitate him. They tried many times but were unable to restart his heart. Finally they located a man who could read Korean, and after reading the card he informed them the Korean corpsman, in the field, had declared the marine dead twenty minutes ago. The doctors and nurses put down their equipment, took off their gloves, and slowly walked away without saying a word as they realized their efforts had been in vain. It had been amazing to watch them work so hard to revive a man who had been declared dead more than twenty minutes earlier.

After I was x-rayed and given more medication, I left the hangar. A chopper landed nearby, and a Marine jumped off of it carrying a poncho. He was carrying the poncho by all four corners in his right fist, and he was holding it out to his side, chest high. There was something in the poncho, but I could not tell what it was. The load couldn't have weighed more than twenty or twenty-five pounds by the way he was carrying it. As he trotted past me, one of the corners of the poncho fell from his hand. To my shock the opening revealed what appeared to be a bloody thigh and some intestines and other body parts. They did not fall to the ground—they just kind of flopped around inside the poncho as he trotted by. It was like he was moving in slow motion with those bloody remains bouncing around inside the poncho. He was headed for the morgue.

The remains in the poncho were all that was left of a marine. It was all that was left of some mother's son. It is strange the things you seem to remember the most. I guess I realized it could have just as easily been me in that poncho. I knew my mother would need to see my body if I were killed. She would have a hard time believing I was really dead if she was not allowed see my body. No mother should ever see her son in that condition, and the military sealed the coffins of many soldiers for that reason. The thought of not knowing for sure if it was me in the casket would have haunted my mother for the rest of her life.

From 1962 to 1971 there were over nineteen million gallons of herbicides sprayed in South Vietnam, most of which was Agent Orange. Agent Orange could be identified by the orange stripe around the barrels it came in.

William L Mott

This was the Bunker on Hill 22

Cpl King on Operation Pipestone Canyon

Loyd Gomez on left and Sgt Hada on right

Charles Butler

Swan's Shop on Hill 55 Miller on the left and Swan in front

William Larry Mott

Me on the left and William L. Mott on the right on Hill 22

PFC Jepsen. Chuck Butlers partner after Gomez

United States Marine Corps

This is to certify that

PFC Jay L. Taylor 2404466/0311/8541

has successfully completed the course prescribed by the Commandant of the Marine Corps for

SCOUT SNIPER SCHOOL

given at:

BASIC INFANTRY TRAINING BATTALION
2nd INFANTRY TRAINING REGIMENT
M.C.B. CAMP PENDLETON, CALIFORNIA

this 19th day of APRIL, 19 68

R. R. Morris, 1stLt, USMC
OFFICER-IN-CHARGE

J. L. Day, LtCol, USMC
COMMANDING

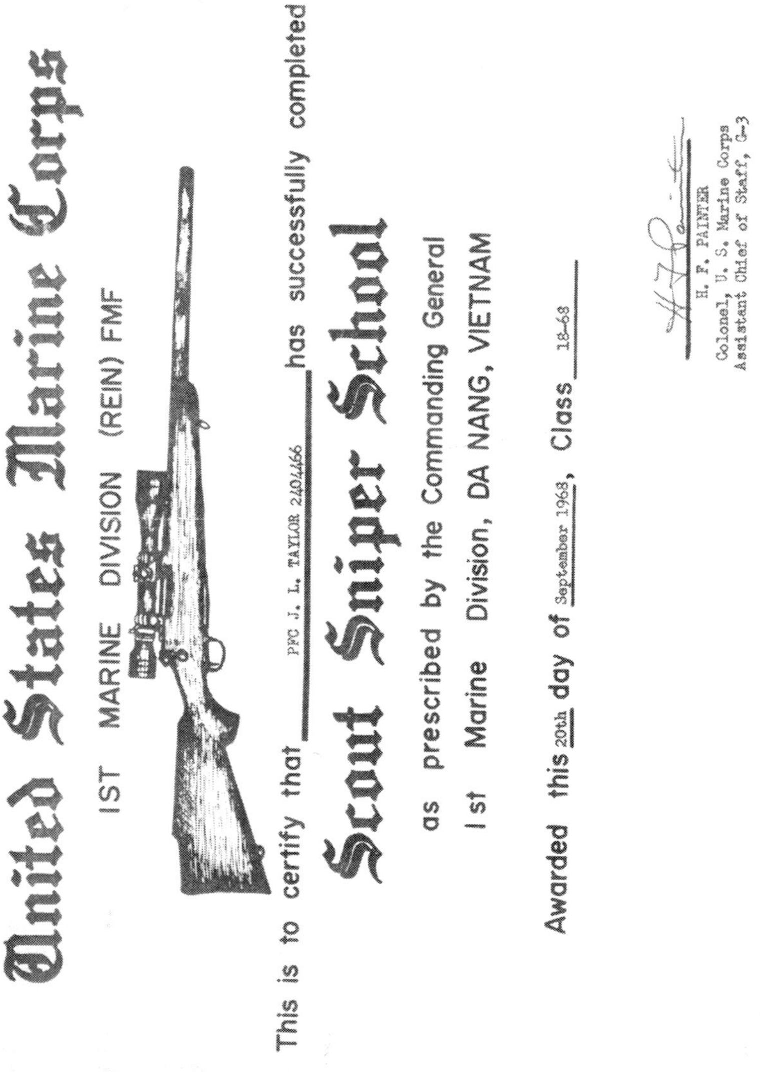

United States Marine Corps

1ST MARINE DIVISION (REIN) FMF

This is to certify that PFC J. L. TAYLOR 2404466 has successfully completed

Scout Sniper School

as prescribed by the Commanding General
1st Marine Division, DA NANG, VIETNAM

Awarded this 20th day of September 1968, Class 18-68

H. F. PAINTER
Colonel, U. S. Marine Corps
Assistant Chief of Staff, G-3

12. Phantom Firefight

On this occasion Mott and I were deployed on bridge guard. There were compounds around all of the bridges in Vietnam, and they were manned by at least a platoon of marines, depending on the size and importance of the bridge. Their job was to protect the bridge so the VC did not blow it up. Grunts would walk back and forth across the bridge all day and night, shooting at anything floating down the river to make sure there were not explosive charges or VC hidden in whatever was floating down the river.

Most of the compounds had a gun tower inside the perimeter. There was also an M50 Ontos stationed at the compound where Mott and I were sent. This was a small tank-like vehicle with three 106 recoilless rifles mounted on each side. The Ontos was also equipped with two 50-caliber machine guns. The Ontos was normally parked under the watch tower located near the center of the compound. Ontos means, "the thing" in Greek, and only 176 were ever made for the Marine Corps. They were taken out of service in 1969.

At this bridge they had been having a problem of trucks being shot at after they had crossed the bridge and left the compound. So far the shooter had not managed to hit anyone or do much damage to the trucks he had hit. They wanted us to spend a few days there and see if we couldn't get this "sniper," as they called him.

Mott and I spent our days in the gun tower watching trucks and jeeps coming in and out of the compound and glassing the surrounding area, trying to locate the shooter. At night we would spend some of our time in the tower glassing for enemy movement with our Starlight scope. Vehicles did not travel the roads at night. They would be sitting ducks with their light on at night and the VC would have the cover of darkness to get in close. In many areas the roads were swept for mines in the morning before traffic was allowed on them.

When we first arrived at the compound, two reporters were there doing a story about the unit guarding the bridge. This did not make the company commander very happy. He did not want the reporters writing an unfavorable article about his unit, and therefore he was being extra tough on his troops. Naturally his troops were anxious to see the reporters return to division headquarters.

On the third night we were there, the grunts had had enough and decided to stage a firefight after dark so the reporters could see some action and hopefully go back to Da Nang. Just before dark, the word was passed around the compound that soon after it got dark one of the grunts on perimeter watch would throw a grenade outside the wire and yell, "Incoming." At that point we would all open up on the hillside across the road from camp. Care was taken to make sure none of the officers got word of the plan. Mott and I decided to stay up in the tower and watch the fireworks.

Sure enough, shortly after dark there was the loud explosion of a grenade outside the wire, and someone yelled "Incoming!" Then all hell broke loose. Everyone started shooting up the hillside—tracer rounds lit up the night. Mott had joined in and was emptying one magazine after another into the hillside. There was a 50-caliber machine gun set up on the roof of the tower, but I had not heard it firing. About that time the 50-cal gunner climbed down through the hatch into the crow's nest and said his 50 was jammed. He grabbed his rifle and started shooting.

Seeing as how I had nothing to shoot except the 700—a bolt-action rifle with a scope on it which was useless at night, I decided to go up and give the 50 a try. Well, I messed with it for a minute or two in the dark and to this day I could not tell you for sure what I did with it, but after re-feeding the ammo belt and chambering a new round I grabbed the handles and pressed the trigger down. It cut loose with a long burst. Before I could turn loose of it, I had tracer rounds going out there two miles and beyond. When I finally managed to get my finger off the trigger, someone yelled up from the ground below and wanted to know if we could see the enemy that far out.

"Hell yes!" I yelled back. "They are everywhere!" Little did I know I was talking to the commander of the Ontos. He then cut loose with those 106s, and their concussion shook the tower so bad it damn near shook me off the roof. I could not get my ass back down through the hatch fast enough.

Finally I think everyone ran out of ammo and it got quiet. I was in many real firefights, and few of them ever expended as many rounds and firepower as this make-believe one had that night. The next morning the two reporters had seen enough, and they packed up their gear and returned to Da Nang. Everyone was much happier; things could finally get back to normal for the grunts.

Two days after the reporters left, we were up in the tower as a truck left the compound and drove up the hill to the south of us. Then we heard the shot. The gunshot came from the right side of the truck, but we had not seen any movement in that area before. I scoped the area with the 700 and Mott was glassing the area with his binoculars. I spotted them at the same time Mott did.

Three hundred yards out from us were three kids, two girls and a boy, running for the nearby village. They were nine or ten years old. The boy was carrying a 45-cal pistol in his left hand, and he had a pistol belt and holster over his right shoulder. They were going from my left to my right, weaving in and out of the tall grass and brush. I could not get a clear shot at the boy, but if I could have, I would have taken the shot. I was concerned I might accidentally hit one of the little girls. I also wanted to make sure that if I did get a shot at the boy, he would fall where we could see the body. I did not want anyone taking the pistol before we could reach the body. A dead kid without a weapon would be big trouble for me.

As soon as I realized I was not going to get a shot before they reached the village, I told Mott to saddle up and we hurried down the ladder to the ground. We ran out the front gate and to the village as fast as we could. I knew what the kids had been wearing and felt sure I could recognize them if we could find them. We started running from hooch to hooch, searching each one as we went. In the fourth hooch we entered, we found the little boy and one of the girls. I grabbed the boy and started questioning him about what he had done with the pistol. He, like most Vietnamese kids, spoke some English, and by this time I had managed to pick up a little Vietnamese. He finally showed me where he had hidden the pistol and belt under a bamboo cot. We then took him and the pistol back to the compound. The CO questioned him for a while and then put him on a truck bound for Da Nang, where he would undergo more questioning.

The little boy had explained to me how he had found the pistol. It was like a game to him to be able to sneak out and shoot at the trucks as they passed by. I don't know if he was lying or not, but I do know if he had stopped for one moment while running back to his village, he would not be alive today; because, I know for sure, I would have shot, and killed that little nine-year-old little boy.

After capturing the "sniper," Mott and I returned to Hill 22, where we continued to go on many patrols. When not on patrol we had some good times. It may be hard to believe that fun could be had in a war-torn, mosquito-infested, hot, and humid country, but we all managed to have fun. Mott was like a big kid. One time when we were on Hill 22 the two of us had a contest to see who could eat the most fried eggs. Mott had read a story in *Stars and Stripes*, a Marine Corps newspaper, about a contest between two marines to see which one could eat the most hard-boiled eggs in one hour. The idea came from the movie *Cool Hand Luke*. That morning at the mess hall we each started out with six fried eggs. We both liked them over easy. When they were gone we returned to the chow line for four more. After eating those we returned for two more at a time until I finally quit. By the time I quit, we had each eaten eighteen fried eggs. I would have puked if I tried to eat one more egg, but Mott sat there across the table from me with that big grin on his face, chuckled, and in his thick Southern accent said, "Jason, I believe I can eat a couple more." And he did.

13. Friendly Fire

Mott and I had been partners for about three months when we were out with Charlie Company. It was a company-size operation. Their captain was on R&R, so the XO, a first lieutenant, was in charge. We had stopped on a finger ridge that overlooked an area known as Sherwood Forest. No one seemed to know why it was called Sherwood Forest, but it was a wooded area and was often full of bad guys, and like other areas, someone had previously tagged a name to it and it had stuck. After the platoon set up a perimeter guard, I asked the lieutenant if we were going to be there for a while. He said yes, the company would stay there until dark. It was three or four hours before sunset, so I let him know that Mott and I were going to go on up the ridge a few hundred yards, and see if we could find a place where we could set up, and watch the canyon floor below. I told him we would return before dark. This was a good area to set up in because it afforded us a large field of fire and there was usually quite a bit of enemy activity here. There was an old tank track right on the top of the ridge, so we got off to the side of it, moved up the ridge a few hundred yards, and found a good spot to hide.

After watching the area below us for a couple hours, we heard a spotter plane behind us, flying over the valley floor on the other side of our ridge. I turned to Mott and said, "Let's go find out what he is looking for." We left our hide and went up on top of the ridge so we could see the valley floor on the other side. We made sure we stayed off the very top of the ridge as much as possible so we would not be sky lined. We found another spot to observe from and started glassing the floor below. As we were glassing the area, the spotter plane fired a white phosphorous round. These "Willy Peter" rounds, as we called them, were used for marking a target; in this case it was marking the target for the two F-111s that were quickly approaching.

We still could not spot any activity on the valley floor. In order to get a better view, we stood up in the middle of the tank track as the jets made their first pass and dropped 500-pound bombs.

As we were standing there still trying to locate what all of the commotion was about, one of the jets passed directly overhead. I did not have a good feeling about this. I said to Mott, "Let's get the hell out of here," and we started to double time it back to the platoon. It was too late, though—the pilot had spotted us.

The next jet was headed our way, and we dove for cover just before the napalm hit. It was so close that the heat was intense. We jumped up and ran some more before the next jet made its pass. Again we dove for cover, and again the napalm just missed us. I looked over at Mott to see if he was okay. He smiled at me, chuckled, and said in his thick Southern accent, "That was pretty close, Jason."

"Shut up and run!" I replied. I was scared shitless, cut and scratched from running through the elephant grass, winded, and sweating like a horse, and he was laughing. We jumped up and ran again. This time we made it to the platoon.

Unbeknownst to us, the lieutenant had called the air strike in on the valley just so he could take some good pictures of the strike. There had been nothing down there. The lieutenant had also forgotten that Mott and I were out on that ridge. The pilot mistook Mott and me for VC and radioed the lieutenant to let him know that there were two VC headed his way.

Just before we made it back to the perimeter the platoon sergeant remembered we were out there and alerted the perimeter guard not to open fire on us. As I saw the lieutenant lying there on the ground with his camera, taking pictures of the jets as they flew overhead, I guessed what he had done. I walked over and stuck the barrel of my 700 six inches from his face so he would have a really good look up the barrel. I let him know there would be severe consequences if he ever called an air strike in on us again. He just looked at me and never replied. He also never pressed charges against me over the incident. I guess he knew if he had pressed charges, he would have to explain why he called in the air strike in the first place. The Marine Corps would probably not appreciate him wasting all that money, and putting all of those people unnecessarily at risk just so he could get some pictures for his scrapbook.

Later, one of the grunts in the platoon told me he could raise five hundred dollars for anyone who could kill the lieutenant. I never considered his offer, yet, little did he know, that I may have done it for free if I thought I could have gotten away with it.

14. Kids and Kool-Aid

The average annual rainfall in Vietnam was forty to eighty inches a year and most of it fell during the monsoon season from May through September. Monsoon season was almost over, but it still had one larger storm left in it. It was mid September, and it had been raining for three weeks. From Hill 22 there was nothing but water as far as we could see. The villagers had to travel in sampans, which were little canoe-like boats the villagers and the VC used to travel the rivers. They used a long bamboo pole to push off the bottom and propel the boat through the water.

When it had quit raining for a few days and the water was subsiding, Mott and I decided we would try to catch a ride to Hill 55 to get paid and collect our mail. We had to walk from the hill to the main highway to catch a ride, and the road from the hill to the highway was covered by four feet of water in most areas.

On our way off the hill, we came across two little Vietnamese girls, about seven or eight years old, trying to get back to their village, but the water was too deep for them to travel through. I didn't know how or why they got there in the first place, but anyway Mott and I offered to carry them across the deep water to higher ground so they could get home. When we reached the dry ground at the main highway and set the girls down, I thought we would get a thank you from them, but instead they offered to sell us some pot. That was most likely what they had been doing at the hill—trying to sell pot to the marines.

What a screwed-up world we were in. These were two little girls who should have been starting grade school, not out selling dope. I wondered if the kids back home were still selling Kool-Aid or picking apples next door to earn their extra money.

Unfortunately over the years the media has painted the picture that we were stoned most of the time while in Nam. How much further from the truth could this be? I know, like anywhere else at the time, there were individuals in Nam who used drugs. Use was more common in some of the rear areas where there may not have been as much imminent danger of enemy attack, but seldom where I was located did I witness anyone using drugs. The few times I did, it was pot and they were not out in the bush when they were using it. When we were in the bush our lives depended on each other, and anyone caught using out there may not have made it back in one piece. Shortly before the end of my tour in Nam and while working on Hill 65, I had a partner who smoked some pot with a couple of the grunts one night. They had the night off, and none of them were on perimeter guard. I guess they thought it was okay since they had not been assigned to hole watch or guard duty for the night, but as far as I was concerned it was for the grunts, not for my partner. The next morning when I was sure his head was clear I told my partner that if I ever caught him using dope again or doing anything else that could tarnish our reputation with Bravo Company, I would kill him. I guess he believed me because I never caught him using again.

In a speech on July 5, 1986, General Westmoreland reported, "There is no difference in drug usage between Vietnam Veterans and non veterans of the same age group." [2]

---

[2] From a Veterans' Administration study and reproduced in a Vietnam Helicopter Pilots Association *Historical Reference Directory Volume 2A*.

15. Heroes and Cowards

We all make decisions every day that could affect us for the rest of our lives. This is especially true on the battlefield. When the enemy is suddenly engaged, you are forced to make decisions that could mean the difference between life and death, and you come out of it convinced that you made the right choices or feeling guilty that maybe you made the wrong choices.

Normally, there were at least three or four teams of snipers stationed on Hill 22 to work with the 1st battalion. Hill 22 was located southwest of Da Nang, between Hill 10 and Hill 41. At the time, Mott and I were one of those teams. We had been running patrols with Alpha, Charlie, and Delta companies. For living quarters the snipers, had been assigned to the first tent next to the road coming up the hill from the front gate. This was what we called home. The tents in this area were stretched over wood frames and had wood floors. The tents were held in place with ropes tied to stakes in the ground on each side of the tent. The stakes were ten feet out from the tent, and the tents on each side of a row of stakes were tied to the same stake. The ropes created a tripping hazard at night if we tried walking between the tents. Most of the time the canvas sides of the tents were rolled up to allow any breeze that might be present to pass through and help keep the tent as cool as possible. When it was not monsoon season, these tents served mainly as shade from the hot sun.

The tent next to ours was used to stage new guys coming into the battalion. They usually stayed there only a day or two before they were assigned to a company. To the south of our tent there was an outhouse, a tank, some perimeter bunkers, and the front gate. Out the back door of our tent was another bunker. Robbie Robinson, Cpl Hanna, LCpl Perry, William Mott, and I were all on the hill on this particular day. We were not scheduled to go on patrol. It was late afternoon, and I had been in the tent cleaning my rifle when a squad of grunts passed by the front door of our tent on their way to the front gate. They were going on patrol for the night. I put down my rifle and walked out the front door of the tent to watch as the last part of the squad left the hill. I saw Hanna walk into the outhouse. There were six or eight new guys in the tent next to us; most of them were not wearing shirts. They were not yet accustom to the heat. It was easy to tell they were new guys—their bodies were Lilly white. They had not been exposed to the hot tropical sun yet.

There was suddenly an explosion in front of me, just outside the wire, and someone yelled, "Outgoing!" (We never did find out who yelled it—it may have been a VC, but I did not see anyone close to the perimeter wire.) I could not see anyone in the direction of the explosion. It sounded to me like a mortar round. The new guys had not come out of their tent but they were also looking in the direction of the explosion. Seconds later another mortar round hit just inside the wire, this time it hit much closer to us. I knew immediately it was a mortar attack, and I spun around and started running between the tents for the bunker at the rear of our tent. One of the first things I always did when we were assigned to a new hill was locate the nearest bunkers to our sleeping quarters and identify the shortest routes to them. I had to jump the tie-down ropes between the two tents as I ran for the bunker.

I could see the faces of those new guys watching me as I ran and leaped over the tent ropes. The new guys still did not have a clue what was happening. It was like I was in slow motion and thoughts were racing through my head. I was terrified of mortar attacks. They were so random and I had no idea where the next round was going to hit, and other than taking cover there was nothing I could but wait till they stopped. I knew I should warn the new guys, but the entrance to the bunker was only big enough to allow one person at a time to enter and I didn't want them to panic and block the entrance before I could get in.

I kept running, and as they watched I started to get mad. Were they idiots? Why didn't they run? More rounds were hitting the hill. Finally I could see the entrance to the bunker and I started yelling at the new guys, "Incoming! Get to the bunker!" A round hit off to my left by the tank and sent a marine who was running for a bunker flying through the air. When I got into the bunker it was dark inside. I could make out Robbie, Mott, Perry, and two other marines. The new guys were right behind me and all made it in.

Mott had also seen the marine get hit by the mortar round, and as soon as everyone was inside he said, "We need to go drag that guy to safety," as he crawled to exit the bunker.

Perry said, "I'll go too," and followed Mott out of the bunker. Robbie quietly followed Perry out. The mortar rounds were still hitting the hill, but fear or not I knew I had to go as well. As I followed them out, I turned to the new guys and said, "Stay here until the attack is over." Just minutes before, I had been too big of a coward to warn those new guys of the mortar attack until I was sure I had a clear path to the bunker, and now I was going back out. Perry, Mott, Robbie, and I sprinted to where the marine was down. He was hit pretty bad. There must have been a dozen small, jagged scrap-metal holes in his chest and abdomen area alone; we decided not to move him. There was no telling how deep the wounds were or how much damage the scrap metal had done. He was conscious, and the mortars rounds were hitting farther up the hill.

I ran back to our tent and grabbed a towel to try to slow the bleeding down. By the time I got back, the mortar attack had stopped and we were calling for the corpsman. The entire attack had lasted only a few minutes and about a dozen rounds had hit the hill. The corpsman was quick to arrive and had brought help, so they took control of the wounded marine. Robbie, Mott, Perry, and I then turned our attention to Hanna. He had gone into the shitter just as the attack started. Sgt Webb showed up—he had been at the top of the hill when the attack started. People were starting to come out of the bunkers, and we were calling for Hanna. We walked over to the outhouse and opened the door, expecting to see Hanna riddled with scrap metal and sitting there on the can, but to our relief we found nothing. In desperation we opened the lid and looked inside to see if Hanna was hiding in the barrel, but no Hanna. Finally we spotted Hanna coming out of one of the bunkers further down the hill. We all had a good laugh at Hanna's expense about looking for him in the shitter.

    I never forgot that incident. I had learned something about myself that was not very pleasant. Bravery did not come natural for me. By not warning them, I had put those new guys at risk of getting hit and maybe even killed, just to ensure that they did not get in my way while I was trying to get to the bunker. It had been a conscious decision at the time to value my life more than theirs. I was able to overcome my fear and go back out during the attack, but I had to have time to think about it and convince myself that I had to do it. My true instinct was for my own self preservation, and I was not very proud of that. I know I have forgotten the faces of many of the people I killed, but I have never forgotten the faces of the young marines in the tent that day as they watched me run past them without a clue of what kind of danger they were in. Maybe there is a little coward and a little hero in all of us.

16. Hanna and the Worm

After we had been on Hill 22 awhile, we were given permanent quarters. It was an above-ground bunker made out of ammo boxes filled with dirt, and we had to put the finishing touches on it. We added a divider wall inside. The roof was made of beams, ammo boxes, dirt, and one of the guys managed to find an old tent to cover the roof. It was real cozy and dry. We had enough space for ten bunks with room to spare.

We soon discovered that by removing the end of one of the ammo boxes in the divider wall and removing the dirt we had a great hiding place for a few bottles of booze. Since we were not allowed to have hard liquor, when we did get it, we had to keep it hidden from the brass.

We had been saving up our hard liquor for a night when none of us would have to go out the next day. Finally the night arrived; none of us were scheduled to go out on patrol the next day. When it got dark we lit the candles, broke out sodas and some C-rations, and carefully pried the end off of the ammo box. There were four bottles of whiskey, one bottle of tequila, and one bottle of scotch. The scotch was Sergeant Webb's. We all poured drinks, made some appropriate toasts, and the poker game began.

Mott and I shared a bottle of whiskey even though Mott did not drink much. Hanna started out with the tequila, and Perry, Robbie, Chuck, Gomez, Tim, and the others passed around the remaining bottles of whiskey. Those who were not playing poker watched. Sgt Webb, being the mother hen he was, sat at the end wall and sipped his scotch. He probably felt one of us had better stay sober just in case the hill got hit.

At midnight the poker game broke up. Most of us were too drunk to stay interested in the game. We were into serious storytelling by then. All of us took turns bragging about our great warrior powers. Sgt Webb still just sat there listening and watching; he had drank very little of his scotch. Mott had quit drinking by now and my bottle was nearly empty and I was now mooching what little I could from the others. Webb's bottle of scotch was starting to look pretty good. I asked Webb for a taste of his scotch, and he was happy to share with me. He said, "You have to acquire a taste for scotch. After tasting it, I let Mark know that if he drank enough tiger piss he could probably acquire a taste for it also. He did not appreciate my assessment of his scotch.

Hanna had a little help with his bottle of tequila and it was now nearly empty. Hanna said he had to go outside and water the flowers, and when he returned he informed us that he had vomited and there was a worm in his vomit. This became a major point of concern, and each of us had to take a turn going outside and inspecting Hanna's vomit. Of course we couldn't take a light with us, so the inspections had to be done in the dark. Each of us had an opinion as to whether or not it really was a worm, and this became the topic of discussion for the rest of the night. Was it a worm or was it something Hanna had eaten?

My bottle was empty by now, so when Webb went outside to inspect the worm, I claimed what was left of his bottle of scotch. By now the scotch didn't taste all that bad. Webb didn't seem to mind much—I guess he thought I would pass out before I could drink very much of it. Maybe Webb was right about me passing out because I didn't really remember going to sleep that night.

I awoke the next morning as everyone else was beginning to stir. All of the bottles were empty, Webb's bottle of scotch included. When Webb discovered his scotch was gone, I was on his shit list again. Since Webb watched over everyone like a mother hen, I actually enjoyed doing little things to keep him stirred up. As we were trying to get over our hangovers, the conversation again turned to Hanna's worm. A few of the brave ones preformed a daylight inspection and the consensus was that it really was a worm. Hanna then got really concerned because he had just extended in Nam and was due to go home on his thirty-day leave in two weeks. If he reported the worm now his treatment might delay his leave. If he didn't report it and get treated, would he pass more worms while he was at home? The final straw was when one of us implied that one of the worms may try to escape while he was at home on leave. We wanted to know how he would explain that to his girlfriend.

Hanna headed for the corpsman's tent. We all anxiously awaited his return. He returned after twenty minutes, and when we asked him what the verdict was, he held up a small, clear pill bottle and a wooden Popsicle stick and muttered, "I gotta get that damn worm so the corpsman can look at it." When we all finally quit laughing, we lined up outside the tent and watched while Hanna, using his Popsicle stick, maneuvered the worm into his pill bottle, all the time gagging and trying not to add to his vomit pile.

We all had a good laugh, Hanna got treated for tapeworms, and he still managed to take his leave on time. It wound up being the last and only chance we all had to let our guard down and drink together.

By this time I had been in Vietnam for over six months. I was eligible for an R&R so I took one. Some of the guys waited longer in their tour to take R&R, but I figured, take it as soon as I could in case I didn't make it. I went to Taipei, Taiwan. I had a great time, I think. I know I stayed drunk most of the time I was there. It was a beautiful country, and the week sure went fast.

After I returned from R&R, Mott and I were split up. I was given a new partner, LCpl Perry, and Mott was paired up with Robbie. They were sent to one of the other hills. A few weeks later word came—William L. Mott, nineteen years old, had been shot through the neck and killed. That night I cried like baby. It was like losing a brother. I know I had not known him for a long period of time, but it was unbelievable how close two individuals could get in a short period of time, especially when our lives depended on each other so much. I know now it would not have made any difference, but at times I blamed myself for his death, thinking if I had been there, maybe I could have prevented it from happening. I never had the opportunity to say good-bye. His body was placed in one of those green body bags, shipped to Da Nang, and sent home for his family to bury.

The dehumanization process was now complete. Now I felt that if I could just kill all of the people in this country we could all go home. I never again felt any emotions when I got a kill. Once my targets were not human, it became very easy. I really did hate them, and I had no sympathy for them whatsoever. Maybe this was necessary to stay sane, if in fact we really were sane.

We had our own saying, and it went like this: "They should take all of the B-52s, fill them full of asphalt, fly over North Vietnam, drop the asphalt, and make North Vietnam the world's largest parking lot. Then we could all go home."

17. Bravo Company

Perry and I were sent to Hill 65 to work with Bravo Company. Hill 65 was ten miles southwest of Da Nang. It was not as large as most of the other hills in the 7th Marine TAOR. Unlike many of the other hills, there was no tower on hill 65. There was a large command bunker on the top of the hill. There was a village at the base of the hill on one side. There was nothing much between us and Charlie Ridge, except bad guys.

Captain Huffman was the commanding officer of Bravo Company. He was a Mustanger—he had worked his way up through the enlisted ranks to become an officer. He had fought in Korea, and someone said he had been an RCA cowboy, but I never did find out if that was true or not. He did have a reputation of being very hardcore, but I think for the most part, the men respected him. He earned at least one Silver Star while in Vietnam. He must have had a bad experience with a previous sniper team because he didn't seem to care for us very much at first. At the time the role of a sniper in a grunt company was still being defined. Because of the lack of role definition, snipers were sometimes misused, and at times some snipers misused the role to their advantage and were not very productive to say the least.

Bravo was running what they called three-day PPB (Platoon Patrol Based) patrols. A platoon would leave the hill and patrol an area for three days. During the days the platoon would either travel as a platoon or each of the three squads would run a separate patrol route and then reunite at a prearranged spot before dark. At night each squad would run separate patrol routes or ambush sites and then meet back up again at daybreak.

The captain's orders were the sniper team was to go on all of the three-day PPBs. This was a grueling three days for all involved. We learned to sleep when we could, on breaks and during rest stops. At the end of the three days, the platoon would return to the hill as the next platoon was leaving. As the platoon we were with was returning to the hill, we would meet the Platoon leaving, and Perry and I would turn around and go right back out with the next platoon. We did this for a month. We did not spend a single night on the hill; we did not get to take a shower, sleep in a cot, or eat a meal in the mess tent for a month. I think the captain was testing us. He wanted to see if we were going to stick it out or if we were going to quit and go back to Hill 55. Perry and I were not going to quit. It was a good area, we were getting some kills, and Perry and I were getting to know the area like the back of our hand. After a month of sending us on patrol, the captain must have decided we were good enough to work with his company, and we were allowed to take a break from the PPBs.

Although the patrols around Hill 65 were going good and we were being productive, Perry and I did not remain partners very long. We were a good team, but when we were not in the bush we did not always get along. I think that was because we were both a little hardheaded. Most snipers were very independent and self confident. We were the best long-range killers in the world and we knew it. Perry should have been a team leader when I first got him—he had enough experience and knowledge to qualify as a team leader. He was one of the better partners I had while I was in Nam. I knew he would always be there if I needed him.

Shortly after Perry and I where partnered up and while we were out on patrol next to the Song Vu Gia River, the platoon we were with had stopped and we were taking a break. It was raining and Perry and I were kneeling on the ground under a poncho attempting to light a cigarette when we heard a shot coming from the other side of the river. Someone shouted, "Corpsman up!" One of the grunts up the line was hit.

Perry looked at me and said, "Sounds like they need us." We stood up, and darting from one clump of grass to the other, we ran in the direction the shot had come from. Along the way we passed grunts hiding behind mounds of sand and clumps of elephant grass, trying to stay out of the line of fire. Perry and I were moving closer to the river's edge to see if we could get a crack at this shooter, and Perry was leading the way. As we neared the wounded marine, a burst of rounds kicked up the sand just in front of Perry's feet. He hit the ground, and so did I. Perry lay motionless in front of me and I thought he may have been hit. I jumped up and kept as low to the ground as possible as I sprinted to where Perry was lying. I dropped to the ground to check on him. I could tell by the look on his face that he knew he had narrowly missed being hit. I told him to wait there for a minute and I would lead. He would have nothing of that.

As I started to get up, he grabbed me by the wrist and said, "It's my job to lead—you follow me," and then he sprinted to the next clump of grass. I followed right behind him and hit the ground next to him. We were now about twenty feet from where the wounded marine lay, and I had a clear view of the opposite river bank.

While I tried to get a shot, Perry and the nearby corpsman ran out and dragged the wounded grunt to cover and started treating his wound. I finally got a quick glimpse of the shooter. He was hiding in the brush. He had stripped the bark off of a bush, leaving the leaves and small branches still attached, and fashioned it into a hat. It was a type of a homemade ghillie suit. It did not work. I took the shot and was sure I hit him, but we glassed the area and could not locate a body. It could have easily been hidden in the brush he had been hiding in.

The grunt had been hit in the butt cheek, and although it was painful he would survive. After his shot of morphine he was a pretty happy camper—he had his ticket home, the million-dollar wound, not fatal and a long way from his heart and head. He wanted everyone's address so he could write them when he got home, which was a sure sign the morphine was working.

We all had to combat our fear, some more than others.

It was estimated that over 100,000 NVA infiltrated South Vietnam via the Ho Chi Minh Trail in 1968. U.S. forces conducted over 150 air strikes each day against the trail in late 1968. The hills that the 7th Marine Regiment manned in the Mekong Delta, south and west of Da Nang, were directly in the path of enemy forces entering the Da Nang area from the Ho Chi Minh Trail.

On November 5, 1968, Richard M. Nixon is elected president of the United States.

Bravo Company Marines on a sweep crossing
rice paddies in Dai Loc District.
Photo courtesy of Bob Nichols and Victor Vilionis

Left to right John Perry, Jay Taylor, Robbie Robinson, and Jim Gularte horsing around on Hill 22

Fred Clay and Lt Hegarty photo courtesy of Kernaa Williams and Victor Vilionis

Claud Alfred (Left) and Bill Martin (Right) in an NVA Compound. Claud holding a NVA canteen.

Hill 10 Aerial View Photo by Terry Dixion,
Tom Hannerman, Victor Vilionis

18. My Gear

First of all, I wanted to be able to travel fast. Secondly, it was important to be able to travel quietly. Last but not least, I wanted to be able to travel and set up without being seen. With this in mind I traveled as light as possible. I did not wear a flak jacket or a helmet. They were bulky, noisy, heavy, and hot. I had a pistol belt on which I carried a 45-cal pistol, canteens (seldom more than two), an ammo pouch, and a pouch for my rifle-cleaning gear. I used a corpsman-type bag or a small pack to carry C-rations, map, a poncho liner, and other miscellaneous items.

I carried between eighty and a hundred and twenty rounds of ammo for the 700. It might not sound like much ammo, but I never came close to running out. A bolt-action rifle with a scope is not a very useful weapon in a firefight. If I had ever run out of match ammo I could have used M-14 ammo—they were both 7.62. At times we took a Starlight scope with us. The Starlight weighed six pounds and had 4 x magnification. My partner would mount it on his M-14 at night. The Starlight magnified the light of the moon and stars, and the images in the Starlight were green and black. It was good for perimeter guard at night for up to two or three hundred yards. One drawback to the Starlight was that it was useless in a firefight at night. Tracers, flares, and artillery rounds would light up the sky too much and render the Starlight useless.

For concealment I wore camouflaged utilities. When I could get them I wore the Korean camouflages. I also wore a green derby-type cloth hat with a three-inch brim. This did not always sit well with company officers and NCOs. Some of them did not like the fact that I was not wearing a Marine Corps-issued uniform.

Dec 24, 1968. During the Christmas holiday it was announced there would be a cease-fire in Vietnam. Well, someone must have forgotten to tell North Vietnam. We were out on patrol and we had set up for a night ambush on Christmas Eve night, and even though it was quiet for us, throughout the night we could hear firefights going on all around us.

Jan 1, 1969. We had been on patrol south of Hill 65 with a platoon from Bravo Company all night, and just before daylight we had set up on top of a small hill. As soon as there was enough light to shoot, my partner and I started glassing the surrounding area. Almost instantly we spotted a column of VC as they were winding their way in and out of the brush along a trail approximately four hundred yards west of us. I picked an open spot in the trail, and the next VC that came through it I dropped with one shot. As soon as I fired, the grunts with us opened up. As I was watching the body of the VC I had just shot to see if one of his buddies would try to drag him to cover, a mortar round hit about fifty yards to my right. We called in artillery on their position as more mortar rounds hit in our vicinity. There I lay in the middle of that firefight and mortar attack thinking, *"What a way to ring in the New Year"*. I sure wasn't looking forward to my last six months in country being like this.

19. Tricks of the Trade

Much of the time it was just me and my partner alone in the bush, hiding and snooping around an area for a target. Our support unit was never very far away, and they were always aware of our location. We often talked to the locals to get information on enemy activity and locations, usually without much success.

We managed to learn a few survival tricks of our own. I had found that when my food supply was running low all I had to do was to find some of the local farmers working in their rice paddies. I could then circle the paddy, undetected by the farmers, and search the brush and trees until I found their lunch. It was usually a mixture of rice, fish, and some type of herb wrapped in a large banana leaf. It was much better than the C-rations. I would then eat part of their lunches and leave some piasters or MPC in return. The piaster, or dong, was the Vietnamese money, and MPC was the military money, Military Payment Certificates. There were also a few places in some of the villages I could buy a bowl of rice noodle soup. The soup was very good, and they had chilies that were as hot as any I had ever eaten in New Mexico. When there was meat in the soup I never asked what kind of meat it was.

I never carried as much water as the grunts. I did not have to carry as much weight as they did, and I usually had more chances to find water. I took chances with drinking water from small streams, and I was not shy about putting a couple Halazone tablets in some pretty nasty-looking water and drinking it. There was always the risk of getting sick from drinking untreated water, and I did manage to get sick from it on two different occasions.

There were other options for getting drinking water. The women in the villages normally kept a small cooking fire burning in their hooches during the day. It was used to keep the tea in their teapots hot. The teapot was a small, round metal pot with no lid, half full of water with one or two tea leaves in it. They would drink hot tea even when it was 110 degrees outside. The women never seemed to mind sharing their tea with us. Maybe it was because we had guns and they didn't.

When I was out in the bush I would often run into kids carrying a small block of ice wrapped in a burlap sack. They would use their hand to roll bottles of Vietnamese soda pop on the ice to keep the soda somewhat cold. I had no idea where they got the ice, but they had it, and for a mere dollar I could buy a lukewarm soda. There were also scattered patches of sugar cane in most areas, and the sweet juice from the cane was helpful when we were thirsty.

We seldom found military-age men in the villages. If we did, they were either in the South Vietnam Army or were physically impaired. We never knew which of the villagers might be VC. At times I would check the women's shoulders for pack marks to see if they had been carrying supplies for the enemy. As much as I tried not to think of these people as human, when I saw the elderly men, women, and little kids and the hardships they had to suffer, I often thought that the Peace Corps should be here instead of us.

On patrol

On patrol thru a village

Me glassing

A young Vietnamese girl while on patrol

L. to R. Gunny, Big G, Hanna, and Bridges

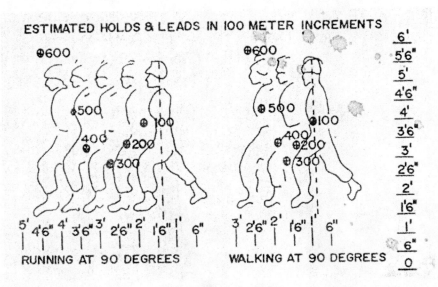
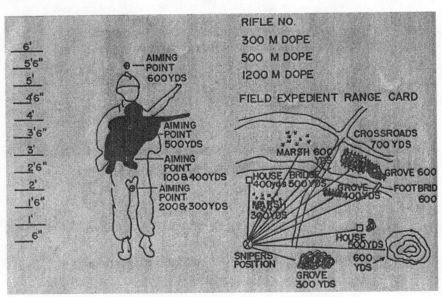

Data Cards that were issued in Sniper School

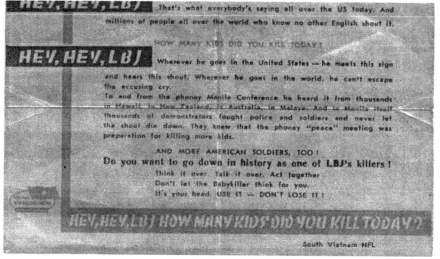

Propaganda leaflets left by the VC and NVA

TACTICAL AIR REQUEST

ELEMENT	EXAMPLE
1. CONTACT	BLUE BIRD THIS IS SNAKE BITE
2. PRIORITY OF MISSION	EMERGENCY, PRIORITY, OR ROUTINE
3. DESCRIPTION OF TARGET	MORTAR POSITION
4. LOCATION OF TARGET	GRID 123456, NORTH SLOPE
5. MARKING OF TARGET	WILL MARK WITH WP ROUND
6. LOCATION OF FRIENDLIES	FRIENDLIES EAST OF RIVER, WILL MARK WITH YELLOW SMOKE
7. DEGREE OF OBSERVATION	TARGET IN DEFILADE, CAN SEE FLASHES, OVER.

PILOTS BRIEFING

1. BEST APPROACH DIRECTION
2. WHEN LAST RECEIVED FIRE
3. WHAT DIRECTION AND HOW FAR ESCORT CAN FIRE
4. SIZE OF L.Z. OR LANDING POINT
5. MARKING OF L.Z.
   a. HEAT TABS
   b. AIR PANELS
   c. FLASHLIGHTS
   d. STROBE LIGHT
   e. FLARES
   f. HAND ILLUM.
   g. SMOKE (DO NOT MENTION COLOR)
6. GIVE PILOT YOUR LOCATION (RELATION TO HELO)

Data cards used for calling in air strikes

MEDEVAC REQUEST

1. PRECEDENCE (EMERGENCY, PRIORITY OR ROUTINE)
2. NUMBER KIA'S, WIA'S, BRANCH OF SERVICE OR NATIONALITY
3. NATURE OF WOUND
4. COORDINATES - 123456
5. L. Z. SECURE OR NOT SECURE
6. MARKING OF L. Z.
7. BEST APPROACH DIRECTION (DEPENDING ON WIND DIRECTION /ENEMY SITUATION)
8. MEDICAL ASSISTANCE REQUIRED
9. REQUESTING UNIT CALL SIGN

CALL FOR FIRE

ELEMENT	EXAMPLE
1. OBSERVER IDENTIFICATION	TINGE GOLF THIS IS SNAKE BITE
2. WARNING ORDER	FIRE MISSION – BATTALION, OVER.
3. LOCATION OF TARGET	GRID 123456, DIRECTION 1230
4. DESCRIPTION OF TARGET	50 VC CROSSING RIVER SOUTH
*5. METHOD OF ENGAGEMENT	DANGER CLOSE, HIGH ANGLE, MIXED, VT, OPEN SHEAF
6. *METHOD OF FIRE	ADJUST FIRE, OVER.

*WILL GET AREA FIRE, LOW ANGLE, HE QUICK, PARALLEL SHEAF IF OMITTED.

Medevac request and Artillery cards

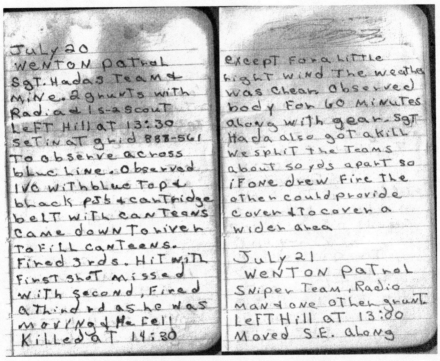

Pages from Chuck Butlers log book. Chuck was one of the few that kept a good log book while in Vietnam.

20. The New Lieutenant

After Perry, I was paired up with PFC James Miller. He was from the Twin Cities area. From that point until I left country many of the new guys coming into the platoon were sent out to us for a few weeks to break in and then were assigned to a permanent partner. At first I didn't care much for Miller, and that was okay by me. I thought, *If he gets himself killed it won't bother me.* Even though he seemed to make a lot of mistakes at first, he did get better, and as much as I tried not to like him, eventually he kind of grew on me.

By now I felt I had the respect of all of Bravo Company. I think they considered me and my partner their permanent sniper team and a part of Bravo Company. The captain and his platoon commanders were using us very effectively, and they were also allowing us to pick many of our own missions.

Shortly after I was paired up with Miller, a new second lieutenant arrived at Bravo Company. We went out with him on his first patrol. Like most new guys in country, he was insecure, scared, and operated strictly "by the book." At first he was unwilling to utilize the knowledge of those who had been in country for a longer period of time, but it didn't take long for that to change.

A week later, Cpl Hanna arrived at Hill 65 with a brand new 700 for me. The one I had been using was not in very good shape. It was a used rifle when I first received it, and the lands and grooves in the barrel were badly worn and pitted. I had not realized how much that had affected its range. After sighting the new rifle in, Miller and I went out again with the new second lieutenant. The platoon left the hill just before dark and headed for the base of Charlie Ridge. Once we reached the base, we humped up one ridge, down the other side, across the creek at the bottom and up the next ridge. This went on all night long until just before dawn, when we stopped on top of one of the finger ridges.

At dawn Miller and I started glassing the ridge across from us for bad guys. Almost immediately we spotted fifteen VC traveling up the next ridge and carrying supplies and weapons. They were eight hundred yards out. With Miller spotting I picked one out, held over, and fired. "You shot high," Miller said. I fired again with the same results.

By now they were all on a dead run. I kept adjusting and finally hit one in the ankle. I hit another one in the arm, and then another one went down. I realized I should have shot my new rifle more before taking it out. I must have taken a dozen shots before all of the targets managed to move up or down the ridge and out of sight. At least three of the wounded, two of which were being helped along by others, were traveling down the ridge to the valley floor below. I grabbed a fire team of grunts and headed down our ridge to attempt to cut them off. As we reached the valley floor, we spotted the one who was hit in the ankle. He was being helped along by another VC. I told Miller to take the helper while I took the wounded one. I took aim and Miller and I both fired. I watched mine go down, but the one with him managed to avoid Miller's fire and escaped into the tall grass. We moved forward until we located the one I had hit.

He had been hit in the right ankle, and there was not much left holding his foot on. The other shot hit him in the small of the back, just left of his spine. He was still alive. Since we did not have a radio with us, medevacing him was not an option. I had made the mistake once before of calling in a medevac for a VC I had shot in the hip. I later discovered that a wounded enemy soldier was considered a priority medevac and therefore would be picked up before a wounded marine. To respond to my medevac call they had actually turned a chopper around that was going to pick up a wounded marine. I never made that mistake again.

I was also not about to roll him over and search him while he was still alive, not knowing what he might be holding under him. He and his partner had been carrying a weapon, and there was not one laying by him now.

As I pulled out my 45, he raised his head and attempted to push himself up off the ground. I shot him in the back of the head. We rolled him over, and sure enough we discovered a chi-com grenade. I had no idea whether he had planned on using it or not, but it didn't matter—I wasn't taking any chances. Killing was not always long distance and impersonal for snipers—sometimes it was very close and vivid. Every time I looked through the scope and pulled that trigger, my intent was to kill my target. This time I had just finished the job.

After searching him and removing the chi-com, we returned to the platoon. We then packed up and were preparing to head back to the hill when the lieutenant asked me if I could take him by the KIA. I knew he had not seen a dead man yet, and I figured we might as well get it confirmed, so I took point and led the platoon to the kill site. We wound our way back down the ridge to the valley floor and back to the location of the kill. The grass around the body was trampled down from when we had first found him and searched his body. The dead VC was covered with dried blood from the bullet wounds in his ankle and stomach and from the fatal wound in the head. There was also dried blood on the ground around him from where we had rolled him over during the search. The flies had found the dried blood and the wounds. There were six or seven of us standing around the body when the lieutenant walked up. Being inexperienced as he was, he looked down at the VC and said to me, "Big one, huh," as if we were deer hunting and I had bagged a trophy.

I replied, "They are all about the same, Lieutenant."

His next comment as he gazed at the body was, "Wow, you shot him right between the eyes," referring to the exit hole in his forehead from the 45 bullet. I guess he chose to ignore the large exit wound in his gut and the ankle wound.

"Not exactly, sir," I replied.

"What do you mean?" he asked.

"He wasn't dead when I found him," I replied.

He realized what I had done and turned very pale. I thought he was going to get sick right there. The grunts standing around us were getting quite a kick out of his reaction, but none of them laughed out loud. He never forgot that day, and from that point on he would often comment to me and others that he thought I was crazy. Before I left Nam I found out for sure just how crazy he thought I was. Maybe he was correct.

"A man is but a product of his thoughts; what he thinks, that he becomes."

Mohandas Karamchand Gandhi

21. What Are Friends For?

I had the opportunity to shoot Charlie while he was performing nearly any task you can think of including while he was bathing, taking a morning stretch, washing his clothes, and once I even shot one while he was squatting down taking his morning constitutional, but the following is one that really stuck in my mind.

It was another hot, humid day, and we had been on an operation with Bravo Company south of Hill 65 in the Thong Duc Valley for the past few days. The night before, Bravo had established a temporary field base and was resting up and waiting for further orders. Miller and I were out scouting and hunting. We were working our way through some dense vegetation and trees, when we came to a point where it ended. We stopped and remained hidden in the brush to glass the area in front of us. Five hundred yards directly in front of us was the Song Vu Gia River. On the far side of the river there was a steep, ten-foot high bank and then a grassy flat area that stretched back another seventy yards to the edge of a thick tree line.

Miller spotted him first. There was a man squatting down on the far bank by the river's edge, washing some clothes. His rifle and pack were leaning against some brush on top of the steep bank. I laid down and got into a good prone position. I had him in my scope; he was 600 yards out. I could place the crosshairs directly on him, point of aim point of impact.

Just as I was about to squeeze the trigger, I noticed movement in the top of my scope. Just then Miller whispered, "There's another one." I raised the scope up and watched as another VC came out of the tree line behind the river. He was walking directly towards the other VC. From where he was he could not see the other VC washing his clothes because of the high river bank. He knew the other one was there—they were probably buddies and he was most likely going to wash his clothes also. Now I had a decision to make. I had a sitting target versus a moving target. I knew the sitting target was a sure thing. If I shot at the one up above the bank while he was walking and weaving his way through the brush, I could miss. Then I would have two running targets. I decided to wait. If the one on top stopped, I would take him first and then try to get the other one before he could get back up the steep bank.

Sure enough, as I was watched, the one walking above the bank stopped. He looked in our direction and I thought he may have spotted us. I saw him look directly at us. Then he looked at the river where his partner was. He still could not see his partner, but he knew his partner was there. As I took aim I hoped I was wrong and he had not seen us. He looked directly at me again, and this time I knew for sure he had spotted us. Before I could squeeze off a round, he whirled and sprinted for cover. To my surprise he never made any attempt to warn his buddy. He didn't yell at him, fire a warning shot, or do anything to alert his buddy—he just ran for his life.

I quickly dropped back down to his partner and squeezed off a round. He was squatted down, and the round struck him in the kneecap. He was done for. The round had shattered his knee and probably a good portion of his thigh. He could not get back up the bank and he could not swim. All he could do was lay there and scream for help. We could hear him clearly from where we were, and I knew his buddy could hear him also. I said to Miller, "Let's wait a few minutes; I want his buddy to remember this for the rest of his life. Besides, maybe someone will try to rescue him."

We must have glassed the area for at least ten minutes, but no one else appeared. I was sure hoping his buddy would poke his head out. At times killing was very personal, and this time that sorry son of a buck deserved to die in my opinion. I knew he was just inside the tree line listening to his partner scream.

I continued to let him scream for a couple of more minutes, thinking his partner was going to have to live with the sound of him pleading for help for the rest of his life. Since we had been spotted I finally decided we had better get out of there before we started taking RPG or mortar rounds. I raised the 700, placed the crosshairs on the wounded man, took careful aim, exhaled, and gently squeezed the trigger. There was to be no rescue for him today. Sometimes they made it real easy to hate them.

It was about this time that I received a letter from home. My mom was good about writing. It always cheered me up to get mail from family and friends back home, especially since it was hard for me to write letters to them. What could I talk about? I couldn't tell them what it was like where I was. They already worried enough, and there was no way they could understand what we were going through without being here.

This was one of those letters none of us ever wanted to receive. In her letter Mom said Mr. Bass had passed away. Mr. Bass had always been so good to me when I was a kid. I had no chance to say my good-byes or attend his funeral. It was just the kind of letter that compounded the stress and helpless feeling of being away from the rest of the world. I couldn't help it—reading the letter made my eyes water and I wanted to cry. What a horribly lonely place this could be. Dad had been in the army during WWII, and he must have known what we were going through, but Mom could only imagine the worst. I cannot begin to perceive what type of hell she must also have gone through for thirteen months.

22. Our My Lai

The My Lai Massacre took place in March 1968, before I arrived in country. It did not become public until November 1969, five months after I returned home. I know now that I worked hard to dehumanize the Vietnamese people so I could kill them without regret. It was my defense mechanism. However, I did not condone the killing or torturing of innocent civilians. The problem lay in knowing who the innocent ones were.

Most of the time when Bravo Company went out as a unit I did not know if we were on a major operation that involved other companies or if it was just Bravo Company on a mission. We were not always aware of the big picture, and we did not need to be. Our world was much smaller. Our world revolved around what was happening now and what we needed to do to survive.

A few weeks after our outing with the green second lieutenant, Miller and I were out with Bravo Company. We were eight clicks (a click was a thousand-meter grid on the maps) south of Hill 65 in an area that was a hot spot for the VC and NVA. It was an area we did not go into with less than full-company strength. In the past we had taken many casualties in this area. There were two villages approximately six hundred yards apart with a small hill in between them. To the west of the villages was a thick tree line, and beyond that was the Song Vu Gia River. Both villages were surrounded by a narrow band of trees and vegetation on the other three sides and rice paddies beyond that. There was a main trail that ran north to south and connected the two villages. According to intelligence reports, these villages were a staging point for Charlie. The villages had been seeded for two months prior with leaflets informing the villagers to leave the area and go to the refugee camp south of Hill 65. At the time, those in the rear who planned these operations determined that all of the civilians had left the villages and only the bad guys were left behind.

Bravo was tasked with sweeping the area on a search-and-destroy mission. We moved in before dawn and stopped north of the first village. The captain wanted us to circle the first village and set up on the hill between the two villages and watch for any Charlies attempting to flee in front of the sweep. There was an air strike scheduled at daybreak to soften up the area in front of the sweep. Miller and I circled the village and set up in a vantage point on top of the hill where we could see both villages. At daybreak I watched as men, women, and children began to stir outside the hooches. None of them showed any sign of knowing we were there. They had no way of knowing Bravo Company was waiting outside of their villages and what was about to happen. I really expected to see some bad guys but I did not.

The jets arrived almost without warning. There were three of them, and they struck one after the other, their bombs striking both villages. The villagers disappeared almost as quickly as the jets arrived. Most of their hooches had bunkers inside them. Some shared a common bunker. Each jet made two passes, and they were gone as fast as they appeared.

Both villages were now dotted with bomb craters and many of the hooches were gone. As soon as the villagers realized the jets were gone, they started to reappear. Captain Huffman had his men launch an E-8 gas canister to chase out any VC that may be hiding. The E-8 had sixteen 35 mm CS gas tubes. CS gas was similar to what most people know as tear gas. Captain Hoffman loved to use the stuff. After launching the gas, Bravo started their sweep through the first village. Without a radio, I had no way of warning them that the villages were full of apparently unarmed civilians. To my surprise only a few rounds were fired before the marines realized there were no bad guys, and the search-and-destroy mission soon turned into a search-and-rescue mission.

As Bravo swept the first village, I watched as people in the other village attended to their wounded and dead. Women and children were crying. There were a group of villagers digging in one of the bomb craters. As they were digging, they were finding body parts.

Each time they found a piece of a body, they would hand it to a young boy who appeared to be about ten years old, and he would climb out of the crater and place the body part in a pile he had started. He would then walk back down into the crater to get the next body part. He appeared to be in a daze. He walked back and forth from the pile to the crater like a robot, showing no emotion while the adults all around him were crying as they used their hands to excavate for more victims.

When Bravo Company completed their sweep of the first village and reached the hill I was on, I went with them into the next village where I had been watching the excavation. I found that little boy and asked him how many people had been killed in the bomb crater where he was working. He told me there were sixteen people missing and they all had been in a bunker where the crater was. He showed no emotion at all. All that was left of sixteen people was a pile of body parts four feet in diameter and three feet tall.

Bravo spent the next few hours rounding up all of the civilians and treating the wounded. Everyone was assembled on the east side of the first village. The captain called in medevac choppers for the wounded who could not travel. We escorted the remaining hundred-plus villagers to the refugee camp near Hill 65.

Our best guess was there had been thirty-five people killed in the villages that day by the air strikes. I struggled with how I felt about this incident. Most of these people were just old men, women, and children trying to survive. On the other hand, I knew these same people had been providing food and shelter for the bad guys. Were they doing it because they were forced to, or were they the enemy also?

Why was it President Harry S. Truman could authorize the dropping of two atomic bombs on Japan, killing as many as 220,000 innocent civilians—men, women, and children—and that was okay? His actions helped shorten the war and save American lives. Was it because our society at the time had learned to hate the Japanese people that much, or had they just dehumanized them? Why was it okay when President Johnson stopped the bombing of North Vietnam, thus prolonging the war and costing more American servicemen their lives? Had the American public learned to hate us that much, or did wearing a U.S. Military uniform make us something less than human?

Over 75 percent of the current population of Vietnam was not yet born when the war in Vietnam ended. Half the current population of the United States was not yet born when the war ended. Currently, eight out of ten Vietnamese think favorably of the United States.

23. Lt Heagerty and the Swamp

Bravo Company had one of the best officers I ever worked with. His name was Lieutenant Heagerty. He was from the East Coast, and he had been a school teacher in New York. He once said to me while we were out on a night patrol, "Taylor, if you think this is bad you should try riding the subway and teaching high school in New York. I have had kids pull knives on me in the classroom." He had been in the Marine Reserve for five years, and when he missed a weekend drill he was activated. He was well liked by all of his men, and he also showed a great deal of respect for them.

About a month after our My Lai incident, we were out on a three-day patrol with Lt Heagerty and his platoon. Miller and I were with the third squad on this particular day. At midday our route took us to the edge of a very large swampy area. We stopped and checked the squad leader's map.

Yes, we were in the correct location, but the route called for us to cross this large swamp which was not shown on the map. According to the map, the area was rice paddies with a small stream running through the middle of them. Years ago something must have caused the stream to dam up somewhere, causing the paddies to flood. I glassed the area, and as far as I could see and there was no good place to go around the swamp. There were a few small hills six or seven hundred yards out on the other side of the swamp. Charlie Ridge loomed behind them.

It was going to be a really bad situation to try to cross this swamp in the daylight. We would be sitting ducks and things were about to get worse. Not realizing how deep the water was, the point man stepped off into it and promptly went in over his head. We grabbed his hands and pulled him back out. We checked up and down the edge of the swamp, looking for a shallow place to cross and could not find one. Finally I volunteered to try. While holding the hands of the biggest grunt I could find, I slid off into the swamp. Luckily, my feet touched bottom and the water was only chest deep. By feeling around with my feet I was able to determine that I was standing on top of an old rice paddy dike. While holding the 700 above my head, I slowly worked my way out into the swamp, feeling for every step with my feet. My partner and the squad members were following behind me at ten-meter intervals. We could see the leeches swimming in the murky water. The going was very slow. I was watching for snakes that might be swimming in the water while also keeping an eye on the hills in front of us for any enemy activity. We had to checkerboard our way across; the dike did not run in a straight line. We really were in a bad situation. If we had been spotted by the enemy it's quite possible none of us would have survived.

Finally after what seemed like an eternity, we reached the hill on the other side. I crawled out of the water and began to help the others out. We wasted no time in moving out—we could pick the leeches off later. I just wanted to get somewhere we had some cover. We found a trail which circled the base of a hill, and we followed it. Halfway around the hill we discovered numerous punji stakes and punji pits. They were on both sides of the trail. The intent was that if we were walking along the trail and the VC ambushed us, we would dive off the side of the trail and impale ourselves on one of the stakes. The traps were not designed so much to kill us as to wound us. Even though the stakes and pits were very old, I did not like traveling the trail knowing the VC or NVA had at one time considered it important enough to booby trap. Finally we managed to get around to the side of the hill and cross over to the next hill, where we met up with the rest of the platoon and Lt Heagerty.

We sat down and began to pick the leeches off ourselves. When we finished we fixed some C-rations and rested. As soon as it got dark, Bravo command began calling in the patrol routes for the night. I was not paying much attention until the squad leader we had been with all day called me over to where Lt Heagerty sat talking on the radio. The route they had called in for his squad to run that night called for them to go right back through the swamp we had crossed earlier in the day.

As I walked up to them, I heard the squad leader tell the Lieutenant, "Ask the sniper. He'll tell you there is no way we can get back across that swamp at night."

Lt Heagerty looked at me and said, "What about it?"

"If you are asking them to go back across that swamp tonight, then you are asking for someone to get killed," I replied.

Lt Heagerty got back on the radio and requested a different route for the squad. He said to Captain Hoffman, who was on the other end, "The sniper lead point through that area today, sir, and he is saying it is too dangerous to attempt to cross it at night."

There was a long pause then the captain's voice came across the radio. "Well, tell the sniper, if he led point across there today he can lead them back across tonight."

Lt Heagerty looked up at me. Without waiting for him to speak I said, "Lieutenant, there is no way I am going back across that swamp tonight. I guarantee if anyone tries to cross that swamp at night someone will get drowned if they don't get killed in an ambush first."

Lt Heagerty stared at me for a minute. I couldn't tell if he was mad at me or just mad at the world for the situation he was in now. He then keyed the mike and said, "Sir, I cannot send my men on that patrol route tonight. Please assign another route, sir."

Instantly the captain barked back, "Are you refusing a direct order, Lieutenant?"

Lt Heagerty replied, "No, sir, I am refusing to send my men on a suicide mission. Please assign another route, sir." There was a long silence and then the company radio man came back on the radio and assigned a new patrol route for third squad. This was why Lt Heagerty's men respected him so much. He held the welfare of his men above all else, including his own career.

All three squads managed to get through the night without any more enemy contact. When we returned to Hill 65 the following afternoon, I was called to the command bunker before I even had a chance to store my gear in the tent. When I entered the command bunker, the captain was already there, standing at the map table in the center of the room. The radio man was sitting at the table against the wall. Captain Hoffman asked me, "Why did you not think we could run that patrol route last night?" He pointed to the map and continued, "There is no swamp there."

I looked at the captain and said, "Sir, I don't care what the map shows. The water across that area is chest deep when I was standing on top of the paddy dikes. We were crazy to have crossed it in the daytime. If there had been any VC on the hills next to the swamp we would have all been sitting ducks. I'll never cross that area again day or night." I braced for his reply. It never came.

All he did was look at me and say, "Okay, you are dismissed." I turned and walked out. To my surprise he had been okay with my assessment of the issue and I never heard another word about it. I don't believe he ever confronted Lt Heagerty concerning the issue either.

24. The Congressional Medal of Stupidity

Miller and I were out on patrol one night with a squad from Bravo Company. Shortly after it got dark, we set up an ambush site in some tall elephant grass that was growing on the edge of the river bank. The patch of grass was long enough to allow all of us to line up along the river bank and watch for enemy soldiers trying to cross the river at night. Miller and I were on the downstream end of the line.

At a little after midnight, the grunt on the far upstream point sprang the bush, opening up on a sampan with three VC in it. They had floated right in front of him in an attempt to reach our side of the river. As soon as he opened up, one of the grunts popped a flare. As the boat floated past, each grunt emptied a magazine or two into the boat and the bodies. More flares were being popped, and by the time the boat had floated downstream to where Miller and I were, the boat was starting to sink and the bodies were rolling in the water. We fired a few rounds into them before the flares burned out and it went dark. It got very quiet again. All we could hear was the water rippling against the shoreline.

That was when my brain must have completely shut down. I shouted to the squad, "Come on, let's get the bodies!" For some reason I had decided the squad should get credit for these kills. Someone popped another flare as I sprinted down river about fifty yards with Miller and the squad following me. I stopped in an open sandy area, stripped my gear off, and asked the grunts if any of them had a K-bar (a knife). One of the grunts handed me his, and I proceeded to wade out into the river until the water was bellybutton deep. I then faced upriver and started looking for the bodies.

At about this time, the cool water must have restarted the flow of blood to my brain. I realized I was the only one in the water. The flare was starting to burn out, and I thought, *What the hell am I doing out here? I can't swim worth a shit; I flunked the swimming test in boot camp. I don't have a gun; this knife is probably duller than a butter knife, and knowing my luck those VC probably aren't even dead.* The last flare burned out and it went dark again. Suddenly, someone or something struck me in the thighs. In a fit of terror I lashed out at the water with the dull K-bar, thrusting it deep into the object that had struck me in the thigh. Before I realized it was the boat, I must have stabbed it at least six or eight times. I was glad that I was standing bellybutton deep in water 'cause I was pretty sure I had just pissed my pants.

As I started to drag the boat to the shore, I could see by the look on the grunts faces that they were quite amused by my thrashing around in the water. It was most likely the first time they had ever seen anyone kill a sampan with a K-bar. I managed to get the boat to the shore, and we recovered some blasting caps, wire, and detonators that had been wrapped in a cloth and stored in the boat. I made no further attempts to wade out into the river to recover anything else. I later cautioned Miller that he was never to speak of this incident to anyone. I am sure that if word of this incident had reached the rest of the sniper platoon I would have been awarded the Congressional Medal of Stupidity. I had sure enough earned it.

During the time I was in Vietnam in 1968 and 1969, our fighting in the Mekong Delta was mainly against the Viet Cong. I would estimate that 60 percent of the shots I took were at VC and 40 percent at NVA. Major battles usually involved NVA troops.

Search-and-destroy missions were very common. The intent was to locate and destroy the Viet Cong and the NVA, their supplies, and their supporters. There were areas which had been designated free-fire zones, meaning it had been determined that there were no "friendlies" in the area. If we spotted anyone in these free-fire zones we were clear to shoot them.

The VC had a very large network of spies and supporters. They could pass as farmers during the day and fighters at night. There were numerous caves and tunnels they used in our area. Many of the women in the villages were either VC themselves or married to VC. The use of children to fight the Americans was not uncommon.

I do not believe the North Vietnamese ever believed they could defeat the U.S. forces. We had complete air superiority. We had artillery support, land and naval, and until the bombing was stopped the B-52 air raids were impacting the supply routes and the North Vietnamese homelands. The NVA troops could not stand and fight a major battle; every time they tried they were soundly defeated. They soon realized that the only way to engage the U.S. forces was at close range with small units that could hit and run and blend in with the local population. Close-range hit-and-run strikes negated our air and artillery support. This type of warfare and the terrain of the Mekong Delta were perfectly suited for sniper warfare.

I believe the North Vietnamese understood that all they had to do was to keep engaging with the American forces, continue to inflict casualties, and wait until the American opposition to the war and the peace talks resulted in a U.S. pullout. When the United States Armed Forces pulled out and later when the United States government stopped financial support of the South Vietnamese Government, the war was over.

25. Read the Signs

The following story is a case of where our scouting ability and knowledge of the land probably saved American lives.

It was late February or early March, and Miller and I were out with a platoon from Bravo Company. We were traveling on an old tank trail two miles south of Hill 65. It was an area we often patrolled, and I had gotten to know it very well. We were approaching a section of the trail where we had been hit many times before while traveling on this trail. I knew that approximately two hundred yards through the trees to our right was a large open area, three hundred yards wide, which paralleled the trail. On the other side of the opening were the foothills of Charlie Ridge. I advised the CO that I thought we should move the platoon off of the trail and through the trees to the edge of the opening on the other side. We could then advance up the valley just inside the tree line and maybe take the VC by surprise. If we didn't take them by surprise, we might catch them trying to cross the opening to get to the foothills. He agreed.

We worked our way through the trees until we reached the opening, and staying just out of sight inside the tree line we continued forward, paralleling the trail. After we had traveled a few hundred yards, I noticed a half-dozen Vietnamese kids herding their cows and water buffalo out of the area. They were in a big hurry. I knew this was not a good sign—there had to be Charlies in the near vicinity. I recognized one of the kids.

I asked the lieutenant to hold the platoon while my partner and I cut across and stopped the kids. The boy I had recognized was one I had talked to many times before. He had always been very helpful and let me know what the VC or NVA in the area were doing. It was obvious he had a real hatred for the VC. I asked him once why he hated them so much, and he said one day he and his mother had been out in an open area by the river when the VC stopped them and some other villagers. While they were standing there being interrogated by the VC, a chopper flew over nearby. The VC ordered them all to get down so the chopper would not spot them. The boy's mother did not move fast enough for them, so they shot her in the head and killed her. I would have guessed the little boy to be around ten years old.

I had my partner move the other kids far enough away so they could not hear what the boy and I were saying. I asked him what was going on. I could tell that he was afraid of something. When I asked him what was wrong, he said if the other kids saw him talking to me and thought he was giving me any information about the VC, they would tell the VC and he would be killed.

I handed him some cigarettes (most of the kids smoked if they could get them) and explained to him that when we were done talking I would hit him and act like I was mad at him so the other kids would think he had not given me any information. He hesitated for a minute, and then he told me there were six VC hiding in the tree line a little further up the clearing. They were waiting there to ambush us. They already knew we had left the road and were moving up inside the tree line. He said they were waiting just past the big bend in the trail. I knew the spot he was talking about.

I thanked him and then slapped him in the face and yelled at him to get the hell out of here. I also kicked and cussed at him as he left. I hoped the other kids bought our act. I hated having to treat him that way. He had always been very helpful and I liked the little guy, and I hoped he understood. I have often wondered if he survived after the North took over.

My partner and I returned to the platoon. I explained to the lieutenant that I would like to go back through the tree line, cross the trail, and try to slip up undetected to the VC's location while he held the platoon at their current location. If I could flank the VC or get behind them I might be able to pick some of them off or at least push them into the open area where the platoon would be waiting for them. The lieutenant was not very eager to let my partner and I go off alone. While I tried to convince him we would stand a better chance of not being detected if we went alone, one of his squad leaders volunteered to go with us. The lieutenant agreed, and the three of us proceeded back through the trees and crossed the trail. Once we were on the other side of the trail, we went far into the brush so we could proceed up to the bend in the trail without being detected by anyone traveling it.

We had moved up about a hundred yards but we were not yet where we needed to be in order to flank the ambush site when we spotted three VC moving in the same direction. They were probably the ones who had been watching the platoon and reporting back to the VC at the ambush site. They were on the opposite side of the trail from us. Two were carrying packs, and the other carried a rifle. As soon as we spotted them they spotted us and started running for cover. We opened up on them and one went down. The other two managed to disappear into the brush.

I was pissed off because we had been detected before we could reach the main ambush site. I really wanted to get those guys. I knew it was the same bunch that had been hitting us every time we traveled this trail. The three of us quickly sprinted to the down VC. It was a woman. She was lying on her back. The bullet had struck her in the back and exited almost in the center of her chest. She was not dead yet, but she was not going to survive much longer.

Although they could not see us from where they were, the VC who had been waiting for us at the ambush site fired a burst of small arms fire in our direction. We quickly searched the tree line for any sign of them but to no avail. I turned my attention back to the wounded VC, and before we had a chance to search her we received another burst of fire from the tree line. This time it was closer, just over our heads. We had to leave. I raised the 700 until it was aimed at the woman's head and squeezed the trigger. What happened next I had not expected. I had never shot anyone from this close a range with the 700, and I had not anticipated how much damage it would do. From that point on I used my 45. We quickly turned, ran for cover, and then returned to the platoon.

The VC were often women. They fought alongside the men, and it was much easier for them to pose as friendly villagers during the day. They also took kids from their villages against their will and used them for packers.

There are veterans everywhere with similar stories who do not feel comfortable talking about them. They keep their memories to themselves to the point where some cannot cope with it any longer. A common belief is one that veterans do not want to talk about their experiences. Much of the time this could not be further from the truth. Most vets really would like to talk about their experiences, but fear how we will be judged by others if we do.

Picture of myself near Hill 22

From L. to R. J.D. Butler, Me at the bottom,
Miller above and Gunny on the right.

River Crossing in Arizona Territory

L. to R. Claude Alferd, PFC Crona a pointman for Mike Company, and Bill Martin

Reinforcements landing

Myself on the left and John Perry at the front of the Sniper tent on Hill 55. Notice the KIA board behind us. It had not been updated since early 1967 at which time 7th Marine SS Platoon had a little over 100 confirmed KIA's and no wounded VC.

Vietnamese Money

26. Partners

I had two partners who did not make it as snipers. One was LCpl Morales. He was twenty-six years old, and he was a native of Puerto Rico. His family moved from Puerto Rico to New York City when he was nine years old. He was new in country when they sent him out to work with me. I really liked him. He was a quiet person, and even though I was seven years younger than him, he had no problem accepting me as the team leader. We only worked together for two weeks before I had to wash him out of the sniper platoon.

We were out on a search-and-destroy sweep with Bravo Company. While Bravo Company was hidden in the trees, the captain deployed Morales and I to a small hill next to the village the company was about to sweep through. The captain told me to shoot anyone who tried to flee in front of the sweep. We were in position for about an hour before the sweep started. It was a peaceful morning. While we were waiting, we glassed the village, watching the children playing outside their hooches and villagers going to work in the nearby rice paddies. Morales made the comment to me that the people and the countryside reminded him of his home in Puerto Rico. At the time I didn't think anything about his comment.

Finally Bravo spread out in a line and began the sweep. I watched as they slowly worked their way through the trees and into the unsuspecting village. Sure enough, as soon they had entered the village, we spotted four VC running out the backside of the village just inside some trees. They were only three hundred yards out, but I knew it would be a difficult shot with them running in and out of the trees. I fired, and while chambering the next round I told Morales to open up with his M-16. I got off two more shots before they got out of sight, and I had managed to drop one of them. Morales never fired a single round. When I asked him why he had not opened up on them, he replied to me that he could not shoot them because they reminded him too much of his own people back home. His earlier statement echoed through my head.

We returned to the company command post two days later. The next day we hitched a ride back to Hill 55. I explained to the platoon sergeants what had happened and told them I wanted a new partner. A few days later, Morales was transferred out of the Scout Sniper platoon. I really felt bad about it, but I knew he would get himself or his partner killed if he had stayed in the sniper platoon. I was afraid he would get transferred to a grunt company, and that would most likely be a death sentence. This part of the job really sucked.

Luckily, two months later I saw Morales again. He was working in the supply room for one of the companies. I felt much better about my decision—at least now he stood a pretty good chance of making it home alive.

The other one was quite different from Morales. I don't recall his name any longer. I only had him for one three-day patrol. He had been in country four days when he showed up on Hill 65. Headquarters had sent him out so I could break him in. After introductions, I let him know we were going on a three-day PPB the next day. I showed him where to stash his gear and told him to get enough C-rations, water, and ammo to last for at least the next three days.

It was not long before he actually informed me that his IQ was much higher than the average marine. He said his IQ was 125, and yet he seemed to have a hard time finding the water tanker and the ammo bunker even though they were both visible from the rack I was laying on in the tent. I had to point the water truck out to him and tell him that if he took his canteen over to it, held it under the little spigot, and turned the handle, water would come out and he could fill his canteen.

When he returned from the ammo bunker, he looked like a Christmas tree with grenades, smoke canisters, and ammo bandoliers hanging all over him. He looked like something out of a B-rated Rambo film. I told him to get rid of all of that shit. All he needed was twelve or fourteen magazines of ammo for his M-16. No grenades! I did not want this green, mental giant packing a grenade around me. Besides, if we were close enough to someone to throw grenades at them, we were too damn close. There were times when I or my partner would carry a grenade or two just in case we found a tunnel or something we wanted to destroy, but I didn't trust this new guy yet.

The next morning we saddled up and headed off the hill. We were not a hundred yards off the hill when I turned around and dammed if he didn't have two grenades attached to his suspenders. Most of us used suspenders with our pistol belts because of all the gear we carried on them. He had run the spoons of the grenades through rings of his suspenders and then bent the spoon over. I guess he thought he was John Wayne. I could just see him hooking the pin of one of those grenades on something and blowing us both to hell.

Now, our trousers had these large pockets on the front of each leg, thigh high. I made him take those two grenades off his suspenders and carry one of them in each of those front pockets for the next three days while we walked through the bush day and night. The grenades weighed sixteen ounces each, and with the pins and spoons rubbing his thighs for the next three days, by the time we returned to the hill his thighs were bloodied and rubbed raw. The next day I loaded him up on a 6x6 and shipped him back to Hill 55. I never saw him again.

Another partner I had for a while was LCpl James Gularte. He was a good partner and I liked him. His dad was an officer in the air force. I would tease Jim from time to time about little things and really get him spun up. He had a short fuse, and just when you thought he was going to blow up, he would burst out laughing.

One night while we were on patrol, Gularte stepped in a hole on top of the rice paddy we were walking on. Charlie would dig holes on top of the dikes—some were ankle deep and some were knee deep. If someone accidentally stepped into one, he could twist or break an ankle or a knee. Gularte broke his ankle that night. We could not medevac him from where we were for fear we might get the chopper shot down. We decided to carry him to more open country before calling in a medevac. The corpsman had a canvas-type stretcher with three handles on each side. We rolled the stretcher out and lifted Gularte onto it. Then, with three of us on each side, we started carrying him to a safer location for the medevac. It was difficult because the dyke was not wide enough to allow us to carry him very well. We had not gone very far when one of the grunts on the handle by his head slipped and lost his grip on his handle. Gularte's head dropped and struck the rice paddy dike. The tops of these dikes could get hard as a rock from all the traffic on them. There was a loud thud when his head hit the dike.

At first I thought he was okay. I decided it would be better if I carried him by myself. I helped him stand up on his good leg, lifted him over my shoulder, and began to carry him. The grunts carried our rifles. We talked as I was walking. After thirty minutes had passed, I could tell something was wrong. He was starting to become incoherent.

We stopped, and after the corpsman examined Gularte he called for a medevac. When his head struck the dike it must have given him a concussion. Before the chopper arrived he went into convulsions, quit breathing, and twice his heart stopped. Each time the corpsman and I were able to revive him. The chopper arrived and we got him loaded. I really wanted to go with him because I was afraid he would quit breathing again on the way to Da Nang, but there was not enough room for me on the chopper.

We returned to Hill 10 the next day and I caught a ride to the 1st Marine Division Hospital in Da Nang, where I met up with Cpl Hanna. We found Gularte in the hospital and visited with him for a while. At the time Jim was unable to remember anything about the night he broke his ankle and sustained his head injury. Jim had a concussion and a badly broken ankle; they were going to rotate him out of country until his ankle mended. Jim was pissed off because they had cut his boot off when he first arrived at the hospital. Our jungle boots had a steel plate embedded in the sole, and it made them very difficult to break in.

Anyway, Jim was adamant that the sorry SOBs should not have cut his boot off, and he was being very vocal about it. He wanted us to get his clothes so he could return to the unit with us. He was not concerned about the broken ankle—he just wanted out of the hospital and back to the unit. His ranting and raving did not go unnoticed, and soon a doctor pulled Hanna and me aside to ask us some questions. She wanted to know if we thought there was anything wrong with

Gularte. I guess she wanted to know if the head injury was affecting his personality. Well, Hanna and I thought he was okay, and I am not sure what we said to her that got her attention, but before Hanna and I could get out of there she was threatening to send a team of doctors to Hill 55 to see if we were all crazy.

As we were leaving the hospital that day, I saw a wounded marine lying in his hospital bed. Both of his legs had been blown off above the knees, and his left arm was missing at the shoulder. When I looked into his eyes all I saw was a cold, blank stare. It was like looking into the eyes of a man whose mind was in another world. I knew for sure if I had walked over to him and handed him my pistol he would have thanked me just before placing it to his head and pulling the trigger. I will never forget the look of despair on that young man's face.

I did not see Jim again until forty years later. I was very fortunate that Jim was the only partner I lost to injury while working together. I also managed to serve my tour without getting wounded.

"One out of every ten Americans who served in Vietnam was a casualty. 58,169 were killed and 304,000 wounded out of 2.59 million who served. Although the percent of those who died is similar to other wars, amputations or crippling wounds were 300 percent higher than in World War II. 75,000 Vietnam veterans are severely disabled."[3]

---

[3] From a speech given by Lieutenant General Barry R. McCaffrey, assistant to the Chairman of the Joint Chiefs of Staff, to Vietnam veterans and visitors gathered at The Wall on Memorial Day, 1993.

27. Olympic Shooter

I didn't care for Hill 55 much even though it was our headquarters. Hill 55 had the best mess hall and conditions were pretty good there, but I liked it better on the surrounding hills with units in the bush—time passed faster there. Occasionally I did have to return to Hill 55 in order to get paid.

Unfortunately, in order to get paid our shot card had to be up to date, and at times it would take a day or two to get caught up on my shots and get paid. On one of these occasions when I was back on Hill 55, Captain Head, our CO, informed us that an Olympic pistol shooter was going to be on the hill the next day and would give us a demonstration of his pistol-shooting ability. They were also setting up some long-range targets, and a few of us were going to demonstrate our marksmanship abilities for him.

The next day we all assembled on a small finger ridge on the east side of Hill 55 where the targets had been set up. We were introduced to a lieutenant colonel. He talked briefly about his accomplishments and then gave a little demonstration of his pistol-shooting ability. Until he pulled out his pistol and started shooting, I really had not been paying much attention to him or what he had to say. I was not much of a shot with a pistol and really didn't see much use for them in combat. Once he started shooting, though, I was amazed. He was by far the best shot with a pistol I had ever seen and still is to this day. When he was done, I and two others took our rifles and shot at the targets that had been set up at 700 and 1000 yards. There was a slight cross wind, but we consistently scored hits at the seven hundred yard target. We were not as successful at the thousand yard target but we did score a number of hits. I think we impressed him also.

Years later I discovered that the man we had met that day was Lt Colonel William W. McMillan, Jr. He was an Olympic Gold

Medalist. He had won the Olympic Rapid Fire Silhouette event in 1960 in a shoot off with two shooters, one from Finland and the other from Russia. He won by firing a 48-50-49 in three series of four to best the other two by 147 to 139 and 135. He also won the 1955 U.S. Marine Corps Service Rifle Championship, among other tournaments.

There were a few competition shooters who successfully made the transition to the snipers, but hunting and killing the enemy had little in common with shooting paper targets. A winning score in our game required coming back alive and unwounded.

28. Longest Confirmed Kill

I know the Scout Sniper of today is better trained, better equipped, and much more effective than we were. Compared to the snipers of today we were primitive cowboys.

Being a good marksman requires a number of things: natural ability, good physical condition, good eyesight, good hand-eye coordination, ability to control your breathing, and ability to control trigger squeeze, just to mention a few. Being a good long-range marksman requires a few more: shoot every day, shoot the same rifle every day, shoot the same type of ammo every day, chose targets at a variety of ranges, and again, shoot every day.

I tried to shoot my rifle as often as possible. If we were on one of the hills for more than a day or two, I would find a spot on the perimeter where I could target shoot, and I would run at least twenty to forty rounds a day through my rifle at different ranges. I shot at rocks, puddles of water, and anything else where I could tell where my bullet struck.

We had been out with Bravo Company south of Hill 65 doing platoon-size sweeps. Miller and I had been set up with a fire team watching an area that one of the platoons had been working. We had been there for four hours without seeing any bad guys. I decided we should move to a new area where one of the other platoons was working in hopes of finding better hunting. The radio man with the fire team notified the CO that we were going to move.

As we were crossing a large open area, Miller spotted something off to our left. It was a lone VC over 1,500 yards out, walking from our left to our right. I was in a hurry—I wanted to get on across the open area. One of the grunts in the fire team said, "Come on, see if you can hit him." I could not lie down and still be able to see him, so I thought, *what the heck, I'll try it off hand.* I raised the 700, located the VC in the scope, and raised the scope until I could barely see him in the bottom left of the scope. I then raised it a little higher until he was not visible in the scope any longer, and I squeezed. The rifle recoiled and then settled back down and I could see him in the scope again. He was still walking. He must have taken at least another ten or fifteen steps when all of a sudden he dropped like he had been hit by a freight train. I couldn't believe it—I had hit him.

The fire team leader got on the radio and called it in. The platoon we had been watching sent a squad to see if they could locate him. We moved to the edge of the open area so we would have some cover and kept glassing the area until the squad arrived at the spot where we thought the VC should be. We could see them searching for the body. Finally they found him and we heard some shots. Then over the radio we heard the squad leader telling the CO they had found the wounded VC. He had been hit in the head, but he was still alive when they got to him and they had finished him off. I heard the captain's voice come on the radio—I could tell instantly he was mad. He did not like that type of talk on the radio.

His voice barked out, "You mean to tell me you found a wounded Victor Charlie and you gunned him down like a dirty dog in the dirt."

There was a moment of silence on the radio, and then the squad leader responded, "No, sir, be advised we found the wounded Victor Charlie that the sniper reported shooting, and when he attempted to flee we opened up with small arms fire resulting in one Victor Charlie KIA."

"That's what I thought you meant," the captain replied. The squad leader marked on his map the location they had found the VC. I marked our location on my map, and I marked the location I thought he was at.

That evening when we linked back up with Bravo Company, the captain, the squad leader, and I compared our maps and range estimates. 1750 yards was the distance at which we put the shot. This was before the time of GPS, and all of our distances reports were a best guess using our experience and the topographical maps. I feel confident it was at least a 1700 yard shot. It was 80 percent luck and 20 percent skill to make a shot like that from a good prone shooting position. It had to be nearly 100 percent luck to make a shot like that from the offhand position. If I had not hit the VC in the head I doubt the grunts would have ever found him. At that range the 308 round had very little energy left in it and the angle of trajectory would have been very steep. I am sure I could try that shot a hundred more times and never make it again.

29. Confirmed Kills

At this point I think I should explain a little bit about how confirmed kills and probable kills were recorded in our platoon during the time I was in country. It was not a very well-defined process and there were no written roles and responsibilities for Scout Snipers at the time. As far as I know, there were no written guidelines stating what was required for a kill to be counted as a "confirmed kill." I am sure this process varied some from unit to unit. In our unit to get a confirmed kill we had to have an officer observe the body after the kill had been made.

When we were on patrol with a platoon or company, there were always officers with the units. Sometimes when we got a kill we would link up with one of the squads and use their radio to locate the nearest officer and have him come to our position to verify the kill. Many times due to the size of the enemy force, the location of the body, or the danger we could incur attempting to reach it, we did not go to the kill site. If the body was visible on these occasions, we would attempt to get an officer to a position where, with the use of our binoculars, he could view the body and verify the kill. There were also times when we were accompanied by a fire team or squad with a radio and they would call in the location of the kill. One of the other squads working nearby the kill site would sweep the area and locate the body for verification.

On many occasions it was just me and my partner out there when we got a kill. We did not carry a radio when it was just the two of us, and we would usually leave to return to the safety of our supporting unit without any verification. In that case it would not be counted as a confirmed kill no matter how dead the target was. When it was just the two of us, we often did not go to the kill site for various reasons, including other enemies in the near vicinity and fear of exposing our location.

Probable kills—I'm not sure just what the hell these were. I guess if we killed someone and could not get it confirmed it could be counted as a probable, in which case, like kills, it would be up to the honesty of the sniper as to how many probables he really had. I never reported a probable kill. The tracking of confirmed kills and probables in our unit's case was very inaccurate at best, and I am sure these guidelines were not applied the same to all units throughout the duration of the war. I think some snipers kept their logs current and may have used them to report confirmed kills without third-party verification, in which case they could be very inaccurate. Again, how accurate these numbers were would depend on the integrity of the individual sniper.

There are reports of some Vietnam-era snipers having very large numbers of confirmed kills. A few may be accurate, but I am also sure many were exaggerated due to the inconsistency of the verification process. The Marine Corps kept no official records of confirmed kills for individual snipers, and therefore there is no way of verifying any claims a sniper may make as to the number of his confirmed kills. Some ex-snipers are like golfers—the more often they retell their stories the worse their memory and math gets.

"The average infantryman in the South Pacific during World War II saw about forty days of combat in four years. The average infantryman in Vietnam saw about 240 days of combat in one year thanks to the mobility of the helicopter."[4] I would estimate the average sniper spent fewer days in the field than the average grunt. Most Snipers saw fewer than 150 days in the field during a thirteen-month tour.

Many snipers spent their entire tours in Nam and recorded less than five or ten kills. This number was certainly not a scale which could be used to judge their worth. Any scale was unfair for the spotter as he did not get credit for confirmed kills while working as a spotter, and yet he was exposed to the same hazards as the shooter

---

[4] From a speech given by Lieutenant General Barry R. McCaffrey, assistant to the Chairman of the Joint Chiefs of Staff, to Vietnam veterans and visitors gathered at The Wall on Memorial Day, 1993.

and oftentimes the team would not have gotten the kill without the spotter.

Getting kills was not our only job. The scouting portion of our job was often overlooked and underrated. We were often sent out in front of units we were working with to scout for the best routes around open areas or to recon for enemy activity. We always traveled with the point squad so we could quickly respond to enemy sightings. At times we observed enemy activity that was out of our range or too close to our hide for us to take a shot. By "too close to our hide" I mean if a large enemy force happened to pass within a hundred yards or less of our hide, it would have been very unwise for just the two of us to take a shot at them. Many of these times the information we brought back was invaluable and saved lives.

We also served as artillery forward observers when we had a supporting fire team and radio with us. At times we took a fire team with us just so we would have the use of their radio for artillery support.

Shot selection is another issue that has been greatly over exaggerated in the media. When we spotted the enemy, they were usually moving and we had very little time to make a decision as to which one to shoot. Here is what I did: I always shot at the one I thought I had the best chance of hitting with the first round. If one was standing still and the others were moving, I shot the one standing still. If one was closer than the others, I chose him. After the first shot the chances of a second kill were greatly diminished. My goal was always to make that first bullet count. I didn't try for head shots. I just wanted to get a bullet in the main body cavity and hope it resulted in a fatal wound.

I have been asked several times over the years if I tried to pick out officers as my primary targets. The answer is I never could tell who the officers were. The VC did not wear rank insignia, and from any distance at all I certainly couldn't tell any difference between one NVA and the one next to him. Therefore, I never wasted a second trying to figure out if someone was an officer or not. If I ever killed an officer it was purely by chance.

The only time I ever thought I might have killed an officer was on one occasion when Miller and I were attached to Bravo Company. We had been working an area south of Hill 10 that consisted of scattered rice paddies with large areas of trees and undergrowth between the paddies. Early that morning, Miller and I, along with a fire team of grunts, set out for an area of high ground that was centrally located in the area Bravo Company would be running patrols that day. We arrived at the spot early in the morning about half an hour before sunrise. It was not a good location to set up in because it only had one way in and out. We were surrounded on three sides by at least fifty yards of deep, swampy water. I decided to stay anyway because it provided the best field of fire for the area we wanted to watch.

The fire team with us was carrying a 30-cal machine gun, so I had them set up thirty yards back up the trail we had come in on to cover our rear and our escape route. At daybreak, Bravo Company started working the area in front of us. We instantly spotted one of the squads from Bravo working its way in and out of some dense vegetation about a thousand yards out from us. Soon we spotted six VC soldiers in a small clearing about six hundred yards out and a little to our right. They appeared to have had spent the night there and were packing up their gear and getting ready to move out. They had no clue we were there and there were patrols working the area all around them. As they got up and gathered their gear, it was apparent that one of them seemed to be doing all of the talking and directing. They had all stopped for a minute and were paying attention to what he was saying when I squeezed the trigger. It was an upper body hit, and he went down like a freight train had hit him. Before I could chamber another round, they were all scrambling for cover. I cranked off a couple of more rounds but I doubt I hit any of them. The one I had shot just lay there—he was dead. He may have been their commander or he may have just been the one telling a good joke that morning. In either case, he was my best target at the time and he paid the price.

Because I was sure the shooting had given our position away, we picked up our gear and quickly rejoined Bravo HQ.

30. My First and Only Chopper Ride

The CH-47 Chinook was a twin-engine tandem-rotor helicopter manufactured by Boeing. It was designed to carry cargo and troops. The original Chinook was designed in 1956, and it had an average cruise speed of 130 knots depending on load and weather conditions. The CH-47A was first used in Vietnam in 1962. The CH-47A had a maximum gross weight of over 30,000 pounds. Over 1,100 CH-47s have been built at a cost of nearly 10 million dollars each.

I only flew in a chopper once while I was in Vietnam, and after seeing one go down, once was enough for me. We were on Hill 10 when we received word that Charlie Company had been hit and needed reinforcements. All of Bravo Company had one hour to get saddled up and muster at the helipad. We were going to be choppered in to reinforce Charlie Company about twelve miles south of Hill 10. They were close to the base of Charlie Ridge, and they had been hit pretty hard. Eight marines had been killed and many more were wounded. When we arrived at the helipad on Hill 10, we were divided into groups of thirty. Each group was staged in two lines of fifteen so when we loaded on the choppers there would be an even number of us seated on each side.

My partner and I were in the third group scheduled to leave the hill. When our chopper touched down, we all ran in to the rear of the chopper in two lines. We had to make sure we held onto all of our gear because the backwash from the chopper blades created a wind strong enough to blow away any light gear that was not anchored down. I was the first one in the chopper in my line, and I went all the way to the front and sat down next to the door gunner. I had the best view for a passenger and could see right out the door gunner's window. Everyone followed close behind me, and as soon as everyone was aboard the chopper lifted off while the rear ramp was being raised.

Landing and takeoff were the most critical times for choppers in Nam, and therefore they did not waste any time on the ground. The flight was a short one, lasting less than fifteen minutes, and most of that time was spent circling in order to allow the jets time to lay down a smokescreen. Because we were landing so close to Charlie Ridge and there was a much higher probability we would receive incoming fire, they had called for air support to lay down a smokescreen between us and Charlie Ridge. I watched as two jets flew by, streaming huge billows of smoke behind them. In a matter of seconds the lower part of Charlie Ridge was hidden behind a layer of smoke, and as soon as the first two choppers had unloaded we headed in for our landing.

On the ground, the first two groups had already started forming a defensive perimeter. The rear ramp of our chopper started to lower, and the crew chief started shouting at us to offload. Since I was now at the back of the line to unload, he was pushing me in the back with his M-14 and shouting at the front of the line to hurry up. I guess now is the point where I should mention that when a chopper sets down in a hot landing zone it does not actually land. It hovers ten or twelve feet off of the ground while the troops jump off. The crew chief continued to push me and shout at everyone to hurry up. I did not realize it at the time, but a critical part of his job as the crew chief was to get us off the chopper as quickly as possible. Each time a grunt reached the end of the ramp he would pause before jumping, thus not allowing the line to move as fast as the crew chief wanted it to and causing him to push and yell even louder. By now I had had enough of him yelling and pushing me, so I turned around to tell him that I was going as fast as I could.

My timing was bad. As soon as I turned around, the two marines in front of me jumped out, and with a big smile on his face the chief gave me one last push and out the chopper I went, backwards, twelve feet down for a hard landing butt first in the elephant grass. Luckily the only thing injured was my pride. I jumped up as fast as I could and threw the 700 up to my shoulder. Looking through the scope, I spotted the crew chief still looking at me with a smile on his face. As soon as he realized I had the 700 trained on him, the smile on his face disappeared and he ducked back out of sight. Now it was my turn to smile. I would not have shot at him, but I'm not sure he knew that.

I didn't have time to stay mad at the crew chief very long. The next chopper was coming and I had to get out of the landing zone. The rest of the choppers got in and out without taking any enemy fire.

Charlie Company had established a perimeter for the medevac choppers on top of a hill one hundred yards east of where we had landed. The base of Charlie Ridge was eight hundred yards to our west. Once all of Bravo Company was on the ground and the perimeter completely set, headquarters was established in the center of the perimeter. It was starting to get dark when they started evacuating Charlie Company's wounded. Our perimeter was in the flight path of the choppers taking off, and this allowed the choppers more time to safely gain altitude while lifting off. Captain Hoffman notified the choppers that we would mark our perimeter with strobe lights. We evenly spaced six strobe lights around our perimeter and turned them on.

Everything went fine as the first two choppers lifted off and headed for the 1st Marine Division Hospital in Da Nang, but when the third chopper flew over us, for some reason the door gunner had not gotten word that we were there and in the dim light mistook the strobe light flashes for muzzle flashes, and he let loose with a burst from his 50-caliber machine gun. The rounds struck right in the middle of our perimeter.

I was sitting on a small mound near the center of our perimeter and Robbie Robinson was sitting next to me. All I could see were tracer rounds hitting the ground all around us. Every fifth round from the 50 was a tracer round. It was over before I realized what was happening. The captain was on the radio screaming for the chopper to cease fire and the corpsmen were running around and calling out to see if anyone had been hit.

Robbie said he had felt a round go by his cheek. I could feel a tingling on the outside of my right leg just above the ankle. When I looked down, I saw a large hole in the right leg of my trousers. My hands were shaking as I untied my trouser cuff. I didn't think I was hit, but at the same time I was afraid my foot was going to fall off when I untied my pant leg. I couldn't see any blood but thought I could feel something on the side of my leg. When I finished untying my trouser leg, I rolled it up. To my relief I was not hit. The same round that had skimmed past Robby's face had gone through the pant leg of my trousers without hitting my leg. The captain had been watching as I rolled up my trousers. Once he was sure no one was hit, he keyed the mike on the radio and informed the chopper pilot that they had just shot a hole through his long rifle's (which snipers were sometimes called) pants leg, and if any of the other choppers opened up on us he would turn his sniper loose on them.

The last two choppers made it out without any further incidents. It had only been a three-second burst, but at six thousand rounds a minute that was at least three hundred rounds fired in a small area with a full company of marines in it. It was a miracle none of us had been hit.

As soon as all the choppers were gone, we saddled up and headed for the top of the hill and what was left of Charlie Company. They had left behind a platoon and eight dead marines. We again set up a perimeter and prepared to spend the night. None of us rested much because we were concerned that the battalion of NVA that had hit Charlie Company might attempt to overrun our position during the night. From where I spent the night I could see the bodies of those eight dead marines. They lay next to each other with ponchos covering them.

The next morning, the remainder of Charlie Company and their dead were evacuated. As soon as the last chopper was out of sight, Bravo began a company sweep of the area. After a short time had passed one of the grunts noticed something did not look right at the bottom of one of the bomb craters. When he investigated closer, he discovered a dead NVA buried in the bottom of the crater. More grunts and Captain Huffman joined him, and when they had completely uncovered the dead NVA they discovered two more were buried under him—except they were not dead. One was an NVA regular, and the other was a twelve-year-old boy. They had no weapons or supplies with them. They had been left to die.

The adult had a compound fracture in his right leg, located halfway between his knee and his hip. The boy's lower lip and part of his chin had been shot off. The NVA and VC did not like to leave their dead behind for the Americans to find, and in this case they had just buried these two alive in an attempt to keep us from finding them. The boy claimed he had been taken from his village against his will two years earlier and forced to pack for the NVA ever since. We questioned the NVA and even twisted his leg a little, but we didn't get any useful info out of him. We called in for a medevac and both of them were sent to Da Nang.

We chased some NVA around for the rest of the day with some light contact a few times that resulted in no casualties for us, and we didn't find any more dead or wounded NVA. I am sure most of the NVA unit which had hit Charlie Company had fled back to Charlie Ridge and were probably watching us as we swept the area. The next day, Bravo Company walked back to Hill 10.

31. Command Decisions

Each time we went through another phase of our Marine Corps training, we met new people. After awhile the faces just seemed to blend together. By the time I got to Vietnam I ran into many grunts I had been in training with, and I often did not recognize them at first. This was the case when I first spotted John Williams. He was a grunt in the second squad, and he had been there a week when I finally approached him and let him know that I thought he looked familiar. It turned out he had joined the Corps much later than I had, so it couldn't have been in training. When I asked him where he was from he replied Florida, but his dad was in the air force and one of the places he had lived was Albuquerque. It turned out we had gone to school together for two years in junior high school. We talked a lot over the next couple of weeks. I did the best I could to fill him in on what had happened to his old friends. I went out on patrol a few times with his squad, and we spent time reminiscing while we were back on the hill. During this time I became friends with John's squad leader and the other grunts in his squad.

About a month after John and I had reunited, we went out on a company-size operation in the Thong Duc Valley. Bravo Company had marched up Route 4 to the Finger Lakes area. The Finger Lakes area was a number of small sloughs filled with stagnant water located about two clicks south of Hill 65 and west of Route 4. Reportedly, there was a large NVA force operating in the area. We did have some light contact with them for the first two days of our operation, and on the third night we had a fairly large firefight. The following morning we found two dead NVA that had not been dragged off. We finished searching the area and then loaded up and headed for Charlie Ridge. The captain felt we were in close pursuit of the NVA and they were headed for the protection of Charlie Ridge.

Miller and I were with John and the second squad, and they were walking point. At noon we reached a small village at the base of Charlie Ridge. The company spread out, and we searched the village. Every hooch was searched and we found nothing. All the villagers we talked to claimed they had not seen any VC or NVA. We did find a well-worn trail leading up Charlie Ridge fifty yards from the village. The decision was made to pursue the bad guys up this trail. John's squad again led point, and Miller and I trailed along behind them with the rest of Bravo Company behind us.

I had been up on Charlie Ridge before, and I knew nothing good was going to come from this trip. It was a well-worn trail we were on, but on each side of the trail was dense jungle forest. In places our visibility was limited to just a few feet, and the canopy was so thick that very little sunlight made it through. In other areas when we walked around a bend in the trail, it would open up and we could see far up the mountain and down into the valley below.

We traveled up the trail for half an hour before we came upon a very large outcropping of rock. There was a large opening under the rock that went deep inside the mountain. It was like a cave. The opening was big enough to fit five or six houses under it. The floor was dirt, and yet it was beaten smooth and shiny like a concrete floor from all of the barefoot traffic on it for the past few years. There were bamboo partitions inside the cave forming a large sleeping quarter and a hospital area. To the right as we entered was a large cooking area. Three hundred NVA could have easily lived there.

As each of us walked up to the cave-like opening we could smell the enemy. It was a pungent odor and made the hair on the back of our necks stand up. We had all smelled it before and knew what it meant. We were very cautious. We knew there had been many of them here and they had not been gone very long.

As we began to search the area, Miller and I walked into the cooking area and saw two one-ton sacks of rice up against the outside rock wall. When we stepped over closer to the rice, I noticed a chicom grenade lying on top of one of the bags of rice. Before I could stop him, Miller reached over to pick it up. I saw his hand reaching for it and knew we were about to die. It had to be booby trapped to be left behind in plain view like that. "No!" I screamed, but it was too late. He picked it up, and to my surprise the world did not blow up. Miller was real proud of his prize until I quit shaking and started chewing his ass. Finally I let up on him and told him to put the chi-com in his pack. It might come in handy later. We finished searching the rest of the area without finding much. We destroyed the rice and headed out again up the trail.

Miller and I were ten or twelve men back from the point man. John was up in front of us somewhere. We were going very slowly. We had only gone about two hundred yards up the trail from the cave when there was a large explosion up in front of us. Instantly everyone hit the ground. I knew someone had tripped a booby trap. From up in front of us came the call for a corpsman. The lieutenant and the corpsman ran past us, and the captain and a couple of others were not far behind them. Miller and I moved up to see if we could spot any enemy activity further up the trail. We came to a small clearing at the front of the column, and there lay John and his squad leader. John had a jagged hole in his calf muscle big enough I could have stuck my fist through it. A large piece of scrap metal had split his squad leader's chest wide open. He had died instantly.

I tried to glass the area up the hill in front of us, but I could not see much. There could have been a hundred NVA hiding up the trail and I would not be able to see them for all the vegetation. I could see most of the way up the ridge, but it would be impossible to spot anyone in the jungle canopy. I could also see the village below that we came through earlier in the day. By now the corpsman had completed putting a bandage around John's leg and the radio man was calling in for a medevac chopper. I heard the captain tell the radio man to call in for an emergency medevac. The corpsman reminded the captain that John's wound did not warrant an emergency. His wound was not critical—it was a routine medevac. I knew the captain would have to call it in as an emergency. If he called it in as a routine they would not send a chopper to Charlie Ridge. It was too dangerous. They would make us return to the valley floor to get the men evacuated. The captain had the radio man call it in as an emergency because he wanted to get these men medevaced ASAP so we could continue our pursuit of the NVA with the hope that we could get them to stand and fight.

Soon we could hear the sound of the chopper approaching. We marked our position with smoke and guided them in. The chopper contained the pilot and copilot, two door gunners, the crew chief, a corpsman, and a hoist operator. There were seven in all. They hovered above us and started to lower a basket for the wounded and dead. This was what the NVA had been waiting for. As the basket reached the treetops the NVA opened up on the chopper with small arms fire. They were up the hill in front of us and probably looking right in the front windshield of the chopper.

We immediately returned fire in their direction as the chopper banked a hard right and headed back down towards the base of the hill and the village we had passed through earlier. Up the hill I could see nothing but trees and vegetation through my scope, and with a bolt-action rifle I was not laying down much of a cover fire, so I turned to watch the chopper. I could tell the flight was unstable, and it appeared the pilot was going to attempt to land next to the village. At least one of the pilots was still alive because someone was flying. They had also managed to hoist the basket back up inside the chopper.

To my horror, as the chopper approached the village they started taking small arms fire again, this time from the village itself. I watched through my scope as the chopper tried to pull up. At first it gained altitude until it was six or seven hundred feet up, and then it was like the tail of the chopper stopped flying. The chopper started rotating and flipping end over end while falling like a rock. I knew all seven aboard were about to die and there was nothing I could do to prevent it. It crashed to the ground in the middle of a rice paddy, and water splashed sixty feet into the air when it impacted. Crashing in the rice paddy probably prevented it from catching fire on impact. Watching through my scope was like I was standing there next to it. I could not see any movement around the crash site. The grunts were still firing up the hill where the NVA had been, and there was no return fire.

I now turned my scope to the village. I wanted to make sure no one from the village or the tree line surrounding the rice paddy was going to run out to the crash site. I knew if there were any survivors and the VC could get to them they would kill them. Two people from the village started towards the chopper, and even though I did not see any weapons on them I lobbed a couple of round in their direction. As far away as they were I stood little chance of hitting one of them, but they didn't know that. They turned and fled back to the village. I watched for a few more minutes, and no one else attempted to reach the chopper.

By now the captain had his men cease firing, and everyone was preparing to head back down the ridge. They were loading the dead squad leader on a stretcher. I remembered what had happened when they had tried to carry Gularte on one of those stretchers, so I volunteered to carry John. The bandage had stopped his wound from bleeding, and he was in pretty good shape other than the fact that he could not walk. We were really in a hurry now to get back down the mountain so we could check the crash site for survivors. I gave the 700 to Miller to carry, loaded John over my shoulder in a fireman's carry, and headed back down the hill with most of the company in front of us.

We traveled down much faster than we had coming up. Each time we got to a place in the trail where we could see the crash site, I would look to see if anyone was there. My two shots must have scared them off because no one else attempted to go to the site.

When we finally reached the valley floor, there were quite a few grunts searching the crash site and removing the dead. Others had already begun to set up a perimeter. A couple of squads were beginning to search the village. As soon as I found a place to set John down, we were told a medevac was on its way. One of the men on the chopper had been thrown clear and was still alive but just barely. They finished setting up a perimeter, and I moved John to a piece of high ground further away from the village that had been established as an LZ (Landing Zone) for the medevac chopper. They brought the dead squad leader, what was left of the bodies of the men who had remained in the chopper, and the injured man who had been thrown clear to join us at the LZ.

When the chopper arrived, they were loaded and the chopper left without taking any more in-coming fire. It was now getting dark and we turned our attention on the village. Martin and Stony had arrived with another unit to reinforce Bravo. We did another sweep and search of the village and still did not find any weapons. We questioned the villagers, and none of them knew anything about who shot at the chopper. We set every hooch in the village on fire. By now it was dark.

Right about then it was a good thing I was not in command. I had just watched seven men get killed. One of them, the squad leader, was a friend of mine. The marine who was thrown from the chopper probably was not going to make it, and I had carried another friend of mine off Charlie Ridge with a hole through his leg that would probably plague him for the rest of his life. As far as I was concerned, the people in this village were responsible for most, if not all, of this loss of American life. The only reason the people in the village that day are alive today is because I was not in charge at that moment. The hatred in me had reached a boiling point.

There I stood on the edge of the village with a number of grunts and Bill Martin and Stony, watching the hooches burn while the villagers milled around them. There was one woman at the hooch nearest to us who was stomping around and yelling in Vietnamese. Unlike the other villagers I could tell she was mad, and she made no attempt to hide her anger from us. I took an instant dislike to this woman. She was mad at us and yet it was her village that shot the chopper down, resulting in the deaths of six American marines.

At that moment I was thoroughly convinced she was a VC and had probably been one of the ones shooting at the chopper. I had never wanted to kill anyone as bad in my life as I did her. If I had had a knife I would have dragged her into the brush and killed her right there and then. I couldn't help it—I was consumed by the hatred I had for these people. For some unknown reason, right then at that point in time I suddenly thought of my mother. What would she think of her little boy now and what had he become? I would rather she see me dead than know what I had become.

Commanders often had to make decisions like the one the captain made that day about whether to attempt to medevac those men from the side of Charlie Ridge or return to the valley floor below and then call for the medevac. They also had to live with the consequences of those decisions. Everyone had their own little piece of hell they had to bring home with them.

32. Politics

6,727,084 tons of bombs were dropped on Indochina during the Vietnam War. Peak troop count in Vietnam was 543,482 on April 30, 1969. Sixty-six percent of the forces in Vietnam were volunteers, compared to WWII where thirty-three percent were volunteers. According to a speech made by General Westmoreland in 1986, 91 percent of Vietnam veterans said they were glad they served, and 74 percent said they would serve again, even knowing the outcome. The U.S. military was not driven out of Vietnam. Congress voted them out.

When I joined the Marine Corps, I didn't comprehend the magnitude of the antiwar movement. I think like many others at that time, I joined because I had a core belief that our government guaranteed us our freedom, and in return we were required to pay our taxes and honor our six-year military obligation. It didn't give me the right to pick and choose and decide if I wanted to participate in the current conflict and whether or not it was a just one. Our elected officials had already made that decision whether I agreed with it or not.

While I was in Vietnam, we were all aware that people in the States were publicly protesting against the war. It angered me. I don't think the protesters realized how much support it gave the enemy or how demoralizing it was to us, or maybe they just didn't care. Returning home was worse yet. Returning vets felt like they were being blamed for the war. There was no welcome home. It was acceptable that many of us had been killed or wounded, and yet we were treated like criminals for having done the same to the enemy. Those who opposed the war took the position that if they were right then we must be wrong, and thus we were the bad guys.

And just so we are perfectly clear on this, Miss Fonda, I have never forgiven you and I never will. In my opinion what you did was treason. Your visit to Hanoi in 1972 and consorting with the enemy during a time of war was inexcusable.

"Those who expect to reap the blessings of freedom must undergo the fatigue of supporting it."[5]

---

[5] *Thomas Paine (1737–1809)*

33. Bronze Star

Many of the stories about snipers depict them hiding for hours and days at a time, waiting for a shot. We did set up in hides, but never for more than a day at a time. Much of the time my partner and I spotted our prey while we were moving.

After I had been with Bravo Company for a couple months, Miller, a new partner we were breaking in, and I were out on patrol with first platoon. We were working an area that I knew very well. I had been out in this area often on the three-day PPBs. We were south of Hill 65 next to the Song Vu Gia River when we spotted twelve VC walking a thousand yards out on the other side of the river. I knew if they stopped I could get a still shot and I could get at least one of them. I wanted more than one, however.

I had been in this area of the river before, and I felt confident we could reach the river bank in front of them undetected, even though there were four or five hundred yards of river-bottom sand between us and the river. There were scattered bushes and grassy areas between us and the river, and it would require using what little cover there was to the best of our advantage. I told the fire team with us to remain where they were, hidden in the tree line, and provide cover fire for us if necessary. I knew we would not have a good escape route, and I wanted cover fire if we were detected.

Then, keeping what cover there was between us and the VC, we maneuvered our way to within three hundred and fifty yards of the them. They were in the river by now and appeared to be taking a little break to bathe. I instructed my partners to hold their fire and spot for me until I was sure of how far I needed to hold under the targets. I knew I had them, but at three hundred and fifty yards and in the water, I could only see their heads and shoulders. I would need to aim at their feet in order to hit them in the chest, so I would have to guess at the location of their feet. We were concealed behind a big clump of river grass, and I was lying down and in a good position. I chambered a tracer round for the first shot. We were not supposed to shoot tracers through the 700 because they were too hard on the barrels, but I wanted to make sure I could tell where the first round hit.

I squeezed the first round off and saw it was just inches high. I had my range, but now they were ducking under the water and trying to float downstream to a point where they could get out on the opposite bank. I kept shooting at heads as they popped up for air. It was like trying to shoot apples bobbing in a barrel of water. It was amazing how long a person could hold his breath when someone was shooting at them. I did manage to hit at least one while they were in the water. Finally they tried to exit at a spot nearly six hundred yards downstream. I stacked them up like cord wood as they stepped out on the slippery bank while my partners were now shooting at two others who had managed to exit the river closer to us and were trying to reach the tree line.

It was over in less than a minute. Only one of them had managed to make it to the tree line. We could see seven dead where they had tried to crawl out of the river and another that my partners had dropped closer to the tree line. It was now time to leave. I knew there had to be others over there, and they were not going to be happy about their losses. Staying concealed as best as possible, we hightailed it out of there. When we arrived back at the safety of the tree line, we glassed the area again and could still see all eight bodies.

The fire team had radioed the first squad, and they soon arrived to see what was going on. The platoon second lieutenant was with them. I handed him the glasses and asked him to count the bodies so we could get credit for the kills.

The lieutenant glassed for a moment and then asked, "How do I know they are dead?" We were now at least eight hundred yards from the bodies. I laid down on the ground and made a rest out of a mound of grass, and then I asked the lieutenant to watch as I pumped a round into each body. Miller gave the lieutenant his binoculars, and he watched the impact as each round struck a body. After I had fired three rounds, the lieutenant said, "That's good enough—they're dead." I cleared the round from the chamber and stood up.

When I did, an RPG round (rocket-propelled grenades—RPG launchers were first designed and manufactured in the Soviet Union and were later manufactured in China and North Vietnam) fired from across the river hit just to the right of us in the tree line. There was a loud explosion, and black smoke, dust, and wood splinters filled the air. I was right—there had been more VC across the river, and they were not very happy about losing their buddies. We fired back with a couple of LAWs and left the area. (The LAW replaced the bazooka. It fired a 66 mm unguided rocket.)

I took credit for five kills and gave my partners the other three. At no time did I feel I was doing anything that took any great amount of courage. I would not have taken my partners to the river's edge if I had not been confident we could get there, kill the VC, and get back safely. For killing eight people I was awarded the Bronze Star. I think it had very little to do with the three of us taking the risk of sneaking up on them—it was the results that counted.

A few days after this incident, I was informed by the regimental sergeant major that I could take another R&R. I was told that the second R&R was in appreciation for the good job I had been doing. It just so happened that Stony was going on R&R at the same time, so Stony and I went to Australia for seven days. Do you know that at that time in Sydney it was legal to serve liquor in a bar for twenty-three and a half hours a day? It almost killed us. Stony had a close encounter with a lady of the night while we were there, but that story is best left untold.

34. Sniper Myths

I have been asked many times if I ever climbed trees for a better shooting advantage while I was a sniper. The answer is absolutely not. I know that WWII movies depict Japanese snipers shooting from palm trees, and although that may have been true it also shows them being shot out of those palm trees. There is only one escape route out of a tree, and it would be very difficult to get into a good shooting position in a tree.

There have been many books written about Vietnam-era snipers and some of them are very good, while others contain great tales of brave and adventurous deeds that make for good reading, but are just simply not true.

There is a story about snipers keeping a company of enemy soldiers pinned down behind a rice paddy dike for days and nights. They picked them off one at a time during the day and used artillery flares to keep them pinned down at night. There are many flaws to this story. First of all, snipers were always attached to and worked in close support with grunt companies. In the case of this story there would have been a grunt company nearby to support the snipers, and they would have responded and destroyed the enemy. It would also not be possible to provide enough light throughout the night with flares to allow a scope or even open sights to be effective.

A two-man sniper team typically did not carry a radio. They relied on the fire team or squad they were working with for radio support, and therefore would have been incapable of calling for artillery support for the flares at night. And last but not least, no commander in his right mind would allow an artillery battery to shoot flares, night after night, at a known enemy location when they could use high-explosive rounds to destroy the enemy instead.

There is, however, an actual event that was reported in the February 1, 1967 issue of *Sea Tiger* about two snipers from 26th Marine Regiment who pinned down a small group of enemy soldiers long enough to allow the supporting grunt company to move into position and capture them. This event took place in a matter of hours, not days.

There are also the tales of individual snipers being dropped behind enemy lines to kill high ranking officers. These stories detail exploits of spending days crawling through the jungle to get into position, and after shooting their target the snipers escape to the nearby awaiting chopper to be flown back to safety. This is another case of a story making what some would consider good fictional reading or the main scene in a movie, but they just simply are not true. There is absolutely no supporting documentation of any event like this ever happening. One of the main concerns of the American commanding officers in Vietnam was to never put any of their combat troops in a position where being captured was highly probable.

"According to Lieutenant General Ormond R. Simpson, USMC (Ret.) who assumed command of the 1st Marine Division in December 1968, when he commented on November 8, 1996, about stories of single snipers who wandered far into enemy territory to "take out" a North Vietnamese Army division commander. According to Simpson: 'First we never had a fix on a NVA Division Command Post. Second if we had we damn sure never would have sent one sniper when we had 176 tubes of artillery and all the possible air we needed. It makes good reading, I suppose, for those never in Vietnam, but it is pure fiction—and not very good fiction,' Simpson said."[6]

There are reports of snipers and other special unit members finding wanted posters. These posters claimed a reward for anyone who killed or captured that particular individual. I know in some cases these reports were true. Miller and I found a couple of bounty posters in an area we had been working. We found a crudely made, hand-drawn poster showing a stick man wearing a derby-style hat, like the one I wore, and carrying a rifle with a scope. The poster indicated there was bounty equivalent to three hundred U.S. dollars

---

[6] *Inside the Crosshairs* by Michael Lee Lanning.

for the stick man with the scoped rifle. Of course I thought it should have been much, much higher.

I know the bounty was not genuine. It was just their attempt at psychological warfare. The VC and NVA also left leaflets calling US troops baby killers and ones that claimed they were written by captured servicemen urging us to surrender to the NVA. I was not near important enough for the North Vietnamese Army to place a bounty on my head, but we were feared by the enemy.

As a unit the snipers did have an impact in the war, and the North Vietnamese commanders recognized it. They attempted to counter with their own snipers, although they were not near as effective as we were. If you are wondering if I kept one of the posters for a souvenir, the answer is no. Remember the rule: "If it didn't grow there, don't f—k with it." When Miller and I came upon that poster that day, the second I noticed it hanging on a tree we backed straight out of the area the way we came in. I had no intention of finding out if it was booby trapped or not.

Two opposing snipers are looking at each other through their scopes, and one squeezes the trigger before the other. His bullet travels hundreds of yards and passes through the other's scope, killing him instantly. This scene has been depicted in movies and stories. I guess one sniper could shoot another thru his scope, but the odds would be very high against it.

The *Encarta Dictionary* defines a sniper as: 1) Hidden shooter—somebody who shoots people from a concealed position. 2) Skilled military shooter—a member of the armed forces who is trained to shoot enemy soldiers from a concealed position.

In most cases an enemy sniper would fit the first definition of someone who shoots people from a concealed position. The North Vietnamese had very few well-trained and equipped snipers. During the thirteen months I was in country, the units I worked with never captured an enemy sniper rifle, though I know a few enemy sniper rifles were captured by other units. Often we took what we called sniper fire only to find out it was a lone VC with an SKS rifle with open sights or someone like the eight-year-old boy with the pistol Mott and I captured while we were on the bridge watch.

While I was in Vietnam we never heard any stories of superhuman snipers. It is hard to believe such stories would surface years later without any hard proof to back up most of the tall tales. It is a shame that in most of these cases, the authors took such liberties with the truth that it robs those who served in the past and those serving today of their true and heroic stories which should be told.

35. The Old Woman and the House

Although I carried a scoped rifle, there were many times we did go out on night ambushes. It was late March, and Miller and I were out with Bravo Company when they received an intelligence report concerning a suspected VC house in our area. The house was just outside a village near the area we were working.

That evening, the commander called me and a squad leader over and reviewed the details of an intelligence report with us. The report indicated there would be a number of local VC meeting at a nearby house that night. The commander wanted to send a squad to the village and set up a bush by the house. He knew I knew the area, so he asked me if I would lead the patrol. It sounded intriguing, so I agreed. We marked the house location on our map, and as soon as it got dark we saddled up and headed out. The house was on the other side of the village from us, so we took our time and skirted around the village. We stayed off of the main trail, traveling alongside of it in the trees and brush. The Vietnamese were not allowed to travel at night, and if we had spotted anyone traveling the trail it would have been VC. Leading point, I took special care to travel slow and make sure we were not detected by anyone in the outlying hooches. It took us about two hours, but we finally reached the house.

It was a large house. It must have been built during the time the French were there. It had adobe-type exterior walls and a wooden porch around the front of the house. The front featured a large, arched wooden door. There were bamboo shutters on the windows. The roof was made of timbers, wood, and bamboo and a three-foot white picket fence encircled the house and yard. It was not the typical hooch. Whoever lived there was an important person.

It appeared to be dark inside. I could not see any candlelight glowing through the cracks in the shutters. We set up in some tall grass and trees thirty yards from the front door. There was a main trail to our left that went to the house and continued to our right towards the village. We had good cover and a good field of fire in front of us and to both sides. Now it was just a waiting game.

There we sat, trying not to make any noise, even when swatting at the mosquitoes. For some reason I really thought we were going to get something that night. Time slowly ticked away. It always seemed to pass slowly when we were on a night bush. A few of the grunts took turns catnapping. One of the first things we learned in Vietnam was how to sleep without snoring. Then, a couple of hours before daylight, someone inside the house lit a candle. The shutters were closed, but I could see the candlelight through the cracks and under the door. We made sure everyone was awake and alert. Maybe now was the time. Still time ticked away and nothing moved up or down the trail. Finally, half an hour before it would start to get daylight; I decided we should go in and see what was going on inside of the house. I whispered to the squad leader and had him send a fire team across the trail to our left so they could watch the back of the house. He was to stay where he was and cover me and Miller while we went into the house. I told Miller that when we reached the house he was to wait on the porch while I went inside.

We slowly crossed the trail, opened the picket fence gate, and made our way across the yard to the front porch. Careful not to make a sound, we crept up to the window next to the front door. When I peeked through the cracks in the window, I could see and older woman kneeling on the floor with her back to us and the door. There was a table in the middle of the room with the candle and what appeared to be some clothing on it. There was a crudely made stool at the table. There was a small wall to the right of the door and I could not see what was behind it. I watched for a few more minutes and was pretty sure she was the only one in the house. I still could not see what she was doing. I motioned to Miller to stay by the window and then headed for the door.

I didn't think I could get the door open without making noise and alerting her, but I tried anyway. To my surprise I was able to slowly open the door until I could step inside without alerting her. My eyes quickly searched the room again. I still feared she might not be alone.

I had a round chambered in the 700 and my finger on the trigger. Slowly I eased forward until I could see around the wall next to the door. There was nothing there, just a bare corner. She was alone.

She was now no more than seven or eight feet from me, and she still did not know I was there. I kept the 700 pointed at her. Now I could see what she was doing. She had four of the wood planks removed from the floor and was going through some documents that had been hidden underneath the floor planks. Some documents were lying on the floor in front of her, and some were still under the floor. There was also a stack of money on the floor. My guess was she had gotten word that she was being watched so she was going to gather up the documents and leave. She was going to pack her documents in the clothing on the table so she could travel undetected.

I still was concerned she might have a weapon or a chi-com under the floor. It was weird being this close to her and her still not knowing I was in the house. I could feel my heart pounding. I took two more steps towards her, and I could now touch her with the 700. Then all of a sudden I knew she knew I was there. I don't think she heard me—I think she sensed I was there. She slowly turned her head and looked at me. I was ready to pull the trigger if she made any sudden moves. She did not.

I motioned for her to stand up and called for Miller. Miller came in and we searched her. We looked through the paperwork and found maps, more money, and documents that we had no idea what they were. We took her outside and gave her to the squad leader, and he instructed two of his men to guard her and shoot her if she tried to escape. We could now see the first faint light of the morning sun. Miller and I went back into the house and searched it from top to bottom. We checked the floor for any other loose boards and found none. We gathered up all of the documents and gave them to the squad leader.

Just to make sure we had not missed any weapons or documents which might have been hidden in the house, we decided to burn it. We piled up anything that would burn, placed in the center of the house, and set it afire. Miller and I stood on the porch and decided we should throw a couple grenades inside just to make sure anything we might have missed under the floor would be destroyed. I stood in front of the window and Miller stood in front of the door.

I had intentionally given Miller the door thinking there was no way he could miss that big of an opening. We pulled the pins, I counted to three, and we each threw our grenades. Sure enough, I heard something rattle around on the porch. I looked down and there was Miller's grenade. Now, I didn't know if he missed the opening or if it hit something inside the house and bounced back out onto the porch—I just knew that it was now lying less than six feet from us.

I don't know why I shouted, "Run!" because Miller had already gotten a jump on me, but I did. I was never known for being a fast runner with my short legs, but on that morning I could have made the U.S. Olympic hurdle team as I leaped the picket fence. I could feel some scrap metal hit me in the ass when the grenade went off. It was a good thing for Miller none of the scrap metal broke the skin or I would not have been the only one to get a Purple Heart that morning. I never again let Miller throw a grenade when I was present.

36. The Perfect Bush

Most of the guys started a short-timer's calendar when they had just two or three months left in country. They would hang up a calendar or carry one with them, and each day they would cross it off and count down until they left country. We would ask them every day how much time they had left in country. I once heard a marine with two days left in country jokingly say, "I got a bowl of corn flakes, a duffel bag drag, and then I'm gonna catch that big bird in the sky." It meant he only had two days left. But it was more than just a joke. As our time got shorter our nerves got worse.

I had less than two months left in country when Miller and I were out on "Operation Oklahoma Hills" with Bravo Company. We were part of a blocking force to stop VC and NVA movement from the Charlie Ridge area. A number of other units would be conducting sweeps in the Thong Duc Valley, and when the NVA or VC attempted to escape across the Song Vu Gia River, we would destroy them. Our part in this operation lasted three weeks.

While we were on this operation, Miller carried an M-14 and a Starlight scope. Bravo Company had set up in a line about a quarter of a mile in length along Highway 4, and we were flanked on both ends by other units to form a line that blocked the VC from escaping across the Song Vu Gia River. Highway 4 was not much more than a grown-over tank trail at the time, and it ran north from the base of Hill 65 up the Thong Duc Valley.

One of the first things we did was clear a good field of fire in front of us. This was an activity I always enjoyed. Using C-4, Bangalore torpedoes, and instantaneous detonation cord, we would blow up all of the vegetation in front of our position. C-4 was a white plastic explosive which we mainly used to clear brush and collapse tunnels. Actually, we probably used C-4 more for cooking our C-rations than for anything else. A small piece placed in an empty C-ration can and set on fire would burn very hot but not very long. It worked great for making a can of coffee. Bangalore torpedoes were invented in 1912 and were used to explode booby traps and barricades and clear obstacles. The Bangalore consisted of pipe sections containing explosive charges which could be connected together. Instantaneous detonation cord was just what the name indicates—it was a white explosive detonation cord that burned at a rate of three thousand yards per second. It could also be used to cut down trees. Five or six wraps around the trunk of an average tree would snap it off like a toothpick. Four or five more wraps would launch it into the air like a missile. Using blasting caps and the instantaneous detonation cord, we would spend hours connecting a combination of torpedoes and C-4 together and placing it in the vegetation that was in our field of fire. Then we would back off to a safe distance, pull the striker, and watch the whole area in front of us explode in a cloud of smoke and dust. When the dust settled we would have a clear field of fire. Where once there had been trees and dense brush, there was now nothing larger than wood chips and toothpick-sized splinters.

After we had cleared our field of fire, we set up our defensive positions using claymore mines and trip flares. Then there was not much to do except wait. During the day we would glass the area in front of us, and other days my partner and I would hunt the area behind our position. The Song Vu Gia River was located five hundred yards behind our defense line. Every few days a resupply chopper would arrive and deliver food, water, and mail.

Because we were often out in the field for long periods of time going from one patrol or operation to another, we sometimes had to wear the same clothing for long periods of time. That was my case then, and as a result of sweat, humidity, and general wear and tear, my trousers were starting to wear and rot out in the crotch area. Since most of us did not wear underwear due to the heat, this was not a good thing, and I had requested a new set of trousers. Each day the hole in the crotch of my pants would get larger, and each day I would greet the resupply chopper, hoping my new trousers had arrived, but they never did. Miller and I could only watch as the others got their mail. We would have to wait until we returned to Hill 55 to get ours.

One night, one of the platoon sergeants who had not been in country very long asked me if I would to go on a night bush with him and one of his squads. Company command had gotten an intelligence report indicating a group of NVA was going to cross the river that night. They planned to hit our line from the rear and attempt to open a hole allowing the NVA inside the box a chance to escape.

I really didn't want to go on a night bush, but the sergeant was very persuasive. He convinced me the intel report was incorrect, as many were, and that it was only a short walk to the river and we would just shoot the bull all night when we got there. I finally agreed.

I knew I had more time in country than him and his squad leader put together, and I appreciated the fact that he wanted me to come along because of my experience. I decided it would be best to leave the 700 with Miller and have him stay at the company defense position. I took his M-14, ammo, and the Starlight.

We gathered our gear and headed out shortly after dark. There were fourteen of us counting the squad leader, the sergeant, and myself. We soon arrived at the riverbank ambush site. There was a small, grassy fishhook of land protruding out into the river about twenty yards, creating a small eddy of water between the main bank and the outcropping of land. I recommended to the sergeant that we set up out there so we would have a better view of the opposite riverbank, and the tall grass would provide good cover. He agreed. After we got set up I started glassing the opposite bank with the Starlight. The river was 150 yards across at this point, and I had a really good view of the bank. There was a large sandbar 150 yards wide before the tree line started. It looked like a beach. I really didn't expect to see anything, but anyone coming out onto the sandy riverbank would be easy to spot. We settled in and swapped stories for the first two hours while I continued to monitor the other side of the river with the Starlight.

Then, as I was glassing, four individuals exited the tree line on the other side and checked up and down the river. Then they returned to the tree line and dragged a sampan to the water's edge. I alerted the sergeant, and he asked if we should open up on them. I said, "No, let's let them get into the sampan and we will catch them in the middle of the river.

As I continued to watch, more NVA began to appear on the river bank with more boats. In just a matter of minutes, there were at least a hundred or more and I knew we did not want to let them get into the river. There would be too many for just the fourteen of us. I checked the map, and we called in for artillery support. I wanted to wait until all of their main force was on the bank before we sprang the bush. I told the sergeant to alert his men to be ready to open fire when the first round hit. The word was whispered up and down to all of the men, "Get ready open up when the first arty round hits."

I continued to watch until the beach was covered with NVA, boats, and gear. I was afraid to wait any longer. I did not want too many of them to get into their sampans for fear many of them would reach our side of the river. We had alerted Bravo HQ about our situation so they could notify the other units in the area. I removed the Starlight from my M-14 because I knew when we popped the bush the light from all of the tracers, artillery rounds, and flares wound render the Starlight useless. I thought, *what the shit am I doing out here? I had less than forty days left in country and I volunteered for a night bush.*

It was time. The NVA were starting to get in the river, so we had the radio man call for the artillery. The first round hit just at the water's edge, dead center of their activity, and we all opened up with our small arms fire while the radio man shouted, "Fire for effect!" over the radio. More artillery rounds followed, one after the other. We could see the NVA running around like a bunch of chickens with their heads cut off. We popped flares and lit up the area, and we could see dead and wounded all over the beach. There was a 30-cal machine gun located five hundred yards upstream and behind us that had a clear line of site to the beach, and they opened up on it also to help support us. Captain Huffman also had a 106 recoilless rifle moved into position upstream for more support. Tracer rounds streaked the night sky.

I could see enemy soldiers dropping as I emptied magazine after magazine into their ranks. I have no idea how many I hit, but I know I got my share. After just a few minutes we were running low on ammo. The sergeant called in for a resupply. We heard the captain on the radio telling HQ Company to get a resupply out to us as soon as possible. We knew it would take them about fifteen minutes to arrive.

I shouted at the sergeant that we needed to pull back and get off of the finger of land we were on—I knew some of the enemy would try to swim the river to avoid the deadly fire we were hitting them with and I did not want any of them who might make it across to get behind us.

We grabbed our gear and pulled back to the main river bank and continued to fire on the other side. The sergeant passed the word for everyone to make sure their ammo lasted until the resupply arrived. I was beginning to worry we might run out of ammo when I remembered that I had left the Starlight on the finger of land. I let the sergeant know that I was going to run back there and get it. He was too busy directing his men to pay much attention to what I was telling him.

I sprinted through the tall grass as fast as I could in the dark. I just wanted to get back out there, find the Starlight, and get back as quick as possible. It was only a short distance, but once I realized I was alone, it seemed like I was miles away. I could hear scrap metal and bullets hitting the water. I could also hear the ripples of water slapping the bank near my feet.

As I neared the location of my Starlight, I suddenly spotted a VC trying to crawl out of the river. He was only five feet away when I shot him; he fell back into the river. If they gave medals for being scared, I would have gotten one. I quickly found the Starlight, and on my way back I shot at two others in the river. When I got back to the squad, the resupply squad was there.

It had only been about twenty minutes from the time we had sprung the bush until the time I returned to the squad, and yet it seemed like hours had passed. Movement on the beach had stopped, and we had walked the artillery further back into the tree line in an attempt to get any of the fleeing NVA.

Soon we could hear a gunship approaching. Spooky, as we called him, flew around for ten minutes, working the area with its guns. Spooky, or Puff the Magic Dragon, was an AC-130 aircraft equipped with 20 mm Gatling guns. The 20 mm Gatling gun was a six-barreled rotary cannon capable of firing more than 6,000 rounds per minute. This was one badass gunship.

When the gunship left, the artillery continued for a while longer and then things got pretty quiet. Using the Starlight, I glassed the beach area throughout the rest of the night. Most of the sampans were gone, either destroyed by the artillery or carried downstream by the river. The sandy beach was dotted with dead bodies. Shortly before dawn we all pulled back to Highway 4.

The next day a Marine recon unit and some units from Bravo crossed the river and searched for bodies. They found a few in the beach area, and more graves were found further back in the tree line. More bodies turned up downriver. A total of seventy-one bodies were found, but from the info that was gathered from local informants it appeared we may have killed close to two hundred NVA with only two minor wounds to our people. Later that afternoon, three helicopters arrived carrying all kinds of big brass. The fourteen of us who were on the finger that night were lined up, and a two-star general, the regimental commanding officer, Regimental Sergeant Major Puckett, the Bravo Company commander, and a few others I did not recognize, inspected our ranks. They stopped at each member of our group and asked questions about the ambush.

About now I was wishing I was wearing underwear. I still had not received a new pair of trousers. When the general arrived where I stood, he stopped and faced me. By now my trousers were torn and rotted from one knee up through the crotch and down to the other knee. So, there I stood facing a two-star general and all of the others standing behind him, with all my manhood visible for inspection. Sergeant Major Puckett ignored it and said to me, "How many VC do you think you killed, LCpl Taylor?"

I replied, "No way of knowing, sir, in the dark and all of the commotion that was going on."

"Surely you have some idea of how many you hit," he replied.

Before I could answer, the general interrupted, he just couldn't stand it any longer. He looked at me and asked, "Marine, can't they get you a new set of trousers out here?" For a second I saw a look of grave concern on the captain's face as he stood there behind the

General. He knew if I told the general I had been asking for a new pair of trousers for the last few days and had not been able to get them, his ass would be in a bind.

I replied, "Well, sir, these just tore last night and the captain ordered me a new pair today; they should be here this afternoon." I could see a look of relief on the captain's face.

The general turned to the captain and said, "Let's make damn sure this marine gets some new trousers, Captain."

"Yes, sir," replied the captain, and then they turned and moved on. I was relieved that I had not had to answer the sergeant major's question about how many VC I had killed the night before, because I had no real way of knowing how many I may have hit, let alone how many I may have killed. At least the general had called me Marine, not son or boy, so I must have passed inspection. A chopper arrived later that afternoon, and on it were my new pair of trousers.

Both the platoon sergeant and the squad leader were promoted and received medals for their part in the ambush. The Bravo Company commander also received a citation. In the after-action report, there was no mention of a sniper being in on the ambush. However, it was mentioned in the report how the Starlight scope had played an important role in the success of the ambush. Because we were always attachments to other units, snipers often did not get credit for the roles they played in the success of the missions.

37. Leaving Country

While I was in country I participated in nine major operations. They were:

1. Operation Allen Brook, RVN—13 May '68 to 17 May '68
2. Operation Mameluke Thrust, RVN—18 May '68 to 08 Aug '68
3. Operation Dodge Valley, RVN—12 Aug '68 to 16 Aug '68
4. Operation Talladega Canyon RVN—01 Oct '68 to 05 Oct '68
5. Operation Maui Peak, RVN—06 Oct '68 to 19 Oct '68
6. Operation Sabine Draw, RVN—28 Oct '68 to 01 Nov '68
7. Operation Lynn River, RVN—27 Jan '69 to 07 Feb '69
8. Operation Oklahoma Hills, RVN—31 Mar '69 to 21 May '69
9. Operation Pipestone Canyon, RVN—26 May '69 to 01 June '69

Most of the snipers in our platoon came out of the field when they only had a month left in country. A few even volunteered for mess duty on Hill 55 when they had a month left in country. Or, for their last month, they might get put on mail duty or they would do nothing and just get ready to leave country.

Time passed too slowly for me when I was not in the bush. Sitting in a compound on a hill was okay for a day or two, but it didn't take long before it got real boring. When my time came and I had only one month left in country, I didn't want to go back to the regimental hill. I thought a month was too long, so I continued working with Bravo Company.

With a little over two weeks left in country, Sgt Hanna paid me a visit at Hill 65. He was delivering our mail and checking to see how we were doing. He wanted to know if I was ready to call it quits and come in out of the field. The thought of getting hit my last two weeks in country was a strong driver, so I said yes.

The next day we hitched a ride back to Hill 55. Soon after arriving on the hill I was informed that Regimental Sergeant Major Puckett wanted to see me in his office. I reported to his tent, and he asked me if I was ready to come in out of the field. Again I said yes. The sergeant major then went on to tell me how he appreciated the job I had preformed while in the Scout Sniper platoon. He even said he thought I was one of the best snipers in the platoon. He then said he would transfer me to Headquarters Company for the last two weeks so I would not have to go out in the bush anymore. I thanked him and turned and left his tent.

As I walked out of the sergeant major's tent, I thought to myself that I may have made some assumptions which weren't correct, but I was hurt and pissed off. I had no intention of transferring out of the sniper platoon. Here I was, in his own words one of the better snipers in the platoon, and he was going to transfer me to HQ Company. They were the ones that burned the shitters on the hill! Now, maybe I would have gotten a cushy job for the last two weeks like working with the armory, mess duty, or being a mail clerk, but all I could think about was burning those damn shitters. I had never even done a single day of mess duty while I was in the Corps, and I was not going to start now. I had trained many of the new guys in our platoon for the last few months, and now he was going to have me burn shitters. Sergeant Major Puckett had lived in New Mexico just like me, and he was going to have me burn shitters. Well, he had another think coming.

On my way back to the sniper tent I had to pass right by the S-1 tent, so right in I went and asked for extension papers. The tent had not changed much since I had left. My old desk was still there along with all the others. The captain who was now in charge of S-1 was the same green lieutenant who had started with Bravo Company. He was the one who thought I was nuts. Well, I got the papers and extended in the Marine Corps for one year and extended in Nam for seven months. I signed the papers right there on my old desk. I would show them—I would take my thirty-day leave in the States and come back and do this some more. They could burn their own damn shitters. I then grabbed my gear and hopped on another truck headed back to Hill 65.

Now, I am not really sure where it started to dawn on me what I had just done, but I can tell you one thing for sure—by the time I got back to Hill 65 the thought of burning shitters was not near so unpleasant.

The next morning I thought, *What the hell did I do?* I could burn shitters standing on my head for two weeks to get out of Nam and the Corps. I couldn't believe I had extended in both. I moped around for the next couple of days feeling sorry for myself and wondering how I was going to break this news to my mother when we got a radio message. The sergeant major wanted to see me back on the regimental hill. Again I hitched a ride back to Hill 55.

I had no idea of what to expect when I walked into the sergeant major's tent. He was sitting at his desk when I entered. He picked up some papers off of his desk and said, "Well, Corporal Taylor, I see here you have extended in the Marine Corps for a year and for another tour here in Nam. The problem is it has been rejected." I couldn't believe what I was hearing. I was getting a second chance.

I'm sure he mistook the surprised look on my face for disappointment. Little did he know I wanted to jump for joy. "I'm not going to beat around the bush about it," he said. "The S-1 officer thinks you are crazy." If that lieutenant had been there I surely would have kissed him. Again I think the sergeant major misread me. "Taylor, you are a good marine and you should consider making a career out of the Corps. If you really want to extend here I can get it pushed through, and I will promote you to sergeant and put you in charge of the sniper platoon. What do you think about that?" he asked. Before I could answer, he said, "Before you answer I want you to go see the career officer and give me your answer tomorrow." I could have given him my answer right then, but I thanked him and politely left.

I was proud to be a marine and I liked being a sniper. The thought of being in charge of the sniper platoon had its appeal, but I had never intended to make a career out of the Corps. I made a quick trip to the career officer's tent, where I listened to his spiel about the benefits of making a career out of the Marine Corps and the $2,500 reenlistment bonus I would receive if I extended for four years. When he was done I thanked him and left. I did seriously think about staying in the Corps. The strong tie to my family was the main reason I chose not to.

The next day I returned to the sergeant major's office and explained to him that I had decided not to stay in the Marine Corps and extend in Nam. He said that was okay and thanked me again for my service. I watched as he tore up my extension papers and tossed them in the trash can.

The next day I hopped a truck back out to Bravo Company, where I remained and continued to go out on patrol until I had only four days left in country. With four days remaining I returned to Hill 55 to pack my gear and prepare to leave country. When my last day finally arrived, I loaded my gear on a truck just like the one I had arrived in thirteen months earlier.

There were very few of my fellow snipers present, as most were out with their respective companies. There was no fanfare, no drawn-out farewells, and no one waving good-bye as the truck left the hill. I was very glad to be going home, yet a part of me was very sad to be leaving what had become my family. I left as I had arrived, alone and afraid of what lay ahead for me.

On June 4, 1969, I boarded a plane in Da Nang and returned home. While I was on the plane I once again realized I was alone. I had left my partners and all of my buddies in Vietnam. They were the only people in the world I had anything in common with right then. I was returning to a world I would hardly recognize. If I was to survive in the real world I was returning to, I would again have to do it alone.

We landed at El Toro Marine Airbase at midnight. Our parents and families did not know the exact time we would return, and therefore there were no family members at the airbase to greet us. I will never forget those people who greeted us that night. There were approximately twenty volunteers there, and they rolled out a red-carpet runway for us as we departed the plane. They stood on each side of the carpet and cheered while they shook our hands. It was the first and only welcome home most of us would ever receive. There were no TV cameras, no crowded airports, no relatives, and no parades—only twenty very special people who were there to welcome us home. They would be the only people to recognize us for many years, and they will never know how much it meant to us.

We were then taken to a large hangar with folding chairs and tables up front, and for the next hour they called each marine who was going to a new duty station up to the tables, issued him his new orders, and released him to go home for his thirty-day leave. By the time they finished issuing new orders, there were about thirty of us left. We were told that we were all considered non-critical MOSs and were therefore eligible for an early out of the Marine Corps. We had our choice: we could go home that night for a thirty-day leave and then be assigned a duty station to serve out our remaining time in the Corps, or we could stay there for the next seven days and be processed out of the Marine Corps. I wanted to go home so bad that night, but I stayed. Seven days later I was released from active duty and met my parents, who had driven out to see me, at the front gate. Mom cried and clung to me all the way home as if she let go of me, I would be gone again. Dad was glad to see me, but he controlled his emotions. If he hadn't we would all have been in tears.

I had been on active duty in the Marine Corps from October 16, 1967 until June 11, 1969. One year, eight months, and eleven days. It would be one year and three months more before I could legally buy a drink or vote for the politicians who had sent us to Vietnam.

April 30, 1975

At 4:03 AM, two U.S. marines were killed in a rocket attack at Saigon's Tan Son Nhut Airport. They were the last Americans to die in Vietnam.

The last American soldier killed in the Vietnam War was Kelton Rena Turner, an eighteen-year-old marine. He was killed in action on May 15, 1975, off the coast of Cambodia, two weeks after the evacuation of Saigon in what became known as the Mayaguez incident.

Others list Gary L. Hall, Joseph N. Hargrove, and Danny G. Marshall as the last to die in the Vietnam War. These three U.S. Marine Corps veterans were mistakenly left behind on Koh Tang Island during the Mayaguez incident. They were last seen together, but unfortunately to date their fate is unknown.[7]

---

[7] www.thewall-usa.com

"The Vietnam War has been the subject of thousands of newspaper and magazine articles, hundreds of books, and scores of movies and television documentaries. The great majority of these efforts have erroneously portrayed many myths about the Vietnam War as being factual. No event in American history is more misunderstood than the Vietnam War. It was misreported then, and it is misremembered now. Rarely have so many people been so wrong about so much. Never have the consequences of their misunderstanding been so tragic."[8]

---

[8] *No More Vietnams* by Richard Nixon

Me with a VC Paymaster that tried to run. We recovered over $500 in Cash and what appeared to be pay records.

A little Vietnamese boy while on patrol. He must have conned one of the Grunts out of a cigarette.

Bill Martin with one of the magazines that saved his life when he was hit in the chest with two AK-47 rounds.

Chuck Butler on left Loyd Gomez on right at their cabin in Colorado. 30 years after Vietnam

7th Marines
1st Marine Division (Rein), FMF
FPO, San Francisco, California 96602

6/GSC/sl
1650
8 AUG 1969

From: Commanding Officer
To: Lance Corporal Charles R. Butler 240 70 32 USMC

Subj: Presentation of Regimental Plaque

1. The Seventh Marines Regimental Plaque is hereby awarded to Lance Corporal Charles R. BUTLER 240 70 32 USMC for outstanding performance of duty.

2. On 23 April 1969, LCpl BUTLER, while serving as a scout-sniper attached to Company K, 3d Battalion, 7th Marines, 1st Marine Division (Rein), FMF, Quang Nam, RVN, during operation OKLAHOMA HILLS, by his superior tactical knowledge, enthusiasm and imagination discovered one 12.7mm Anti-Aircraft Gun with complete tripod assemblies and attachments. This find not only deprived the enemy of the use of this weapon but materially reduced his combat capability. LCpl BUTLER's actions were in keeping with the highest traditions of the U.S. Naval Service and the United States Marine Service.

Gildo S. CODISPOTI

Chuck Butler and Lloyd Gomez each received this citation for their actions during Oklahoma Hills Operation

<u>**YOU'RE ON YOUR OWN NOW!**</u>
<u>But Here Are Some Things to Remember</u>

1. Report to your Draft Board within 10 days.
2. Get out of uniform as soon as possible.
3. Send your insurance premiums monthly to: Collection Subdivision, Veterans Administration, Washington 25, D. C.
4. See your previous employer within 90 days if you want your old job back.
5. Register your Discharge Certificate at the County Court House and get photostatic copies of it.
6. See your Draft Board if you have trouble getting your old job back.
7. See the U. S. Employment Service if you want a new job.
8. See the Veterans Administration about pensions, claims, insurance, etc.

<u>**GOODBYE AND GOOD LUCK**</u>

This is a copy of our Goodbye instructions from the U.S. Government. Note item # 2 it sounded like they were ashamed of us. We really were Disposable Warriors.

The Secretary of the Navy takes pleasure in presenting the MERITORIOUS
UNIT COMMENDATION to
FIRST BATTALION, SEVENTH MARINES
for service as set forth in the following:
CITATION:
For meritorious service in action against Communist forces in Quang Nam Province, Republic of Vietnam, from 21 April to 2 May 1969. The First Battalion, 7th Marines distinguished itself by inflecting heavy losses on North Vietnamese Army units through a series of masterly conceived and skillfully executed tactical moves. In anticipation of heavy enemy movement on the night of 21 April 1969, the battalion head deployed to ambush enemy forces wherever they might attempt to cross the Vu Gia River. Late at night, elements of the battalion observed enemy movement, but held their fire in anticipation of a larger enemy force. The decision proved to be remunerative when a short time later 150 to 200 North Vietnamese soldiers began crossing the river at the ambush position. Waiting until the enemy was in the middle of the river, the battalion initiated the ambush with a devastating volume of fire in a classic ambush situation. The outstanding fire and concealment discipline, and the superb integration of supporting arms brought down 57 North Vietnamese soldiers on the field of battle. An additional 14 bodies were found in shallow graves during the subsequent sweep the next day. Other casualties of the action might have been swept away by the strong river current. An enemy buildup in the same vicinity a week later was outflanked and routed by the skillful use of supporting arms by the First Battalion, Seventh Marines. By their outstanding professional knowledge, tactical skill, and aggressive fighting spirit, the men of the First Battalion, Seventh Marines succeeded in inflicting disproportionately heavy casualties on the Communist forces. In achieving these results, the battalion displayed exceptional qualities of individual fighting skill, indomitable courage, and unit esprit which were in keeping with the highest traditions of the Marine Corps and the United States Naval Service.

For the Secretary of the Navy,
Signed/LEONARD F. CHAPMAN
Commandant of the Marine Corps

1/7 Unit Citation for the April 21st night ambush

Point of Aim Point of Impact

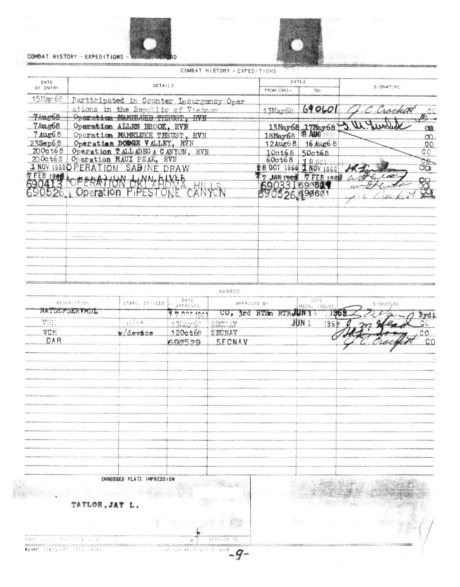

COMBAT HISTORY - EXPEDITIONS

DATE OF ENTRY	DETAILS	DATES FROM (ON)	TO	SIGNATURE
15May68	Participated in Counter Insurgency Operations in the Republic of Vietnam	13May68	690601	J.C. Crockett CO
7Aug68	Operation MAMELUKE THRUST, RVN			CO
7Aug68	Operation ALLEN BROOK, RVN	13May68	17May68	CO
7Aug68	Operation MAMELUKE THRUST, RVN	18May68	8 AUG	CO
23Sep68	Operation DODGE VALLEY, RVN	12Aug68	16Aug68	CO
20Oct68	Operation TALLADEGA CANYON, RVN	10Oct68	5Oct68	CO
20Oct68	Operation MAUI PEAK, RVN	6Oct68	19Oct	CO
1 NOV 1968	OPERATION SABINE DRAW	18 OCT 1968	1 NOV 1968	CO
7 FEB 1969	OPERATION LINN RIVER	7 JAN 1969	7 FEB 1969	CO
690413	OPERATION OKLAHOMA HILLS	690331	690521	CO
690526	Operation PIPESTONE CANYON	690526	690601	J.C. Crockett CO

AWARDS

DESCRIPTION	STARS, DEVICES	DATE APPROVED	APPROVED BY	DATE MEDAL ISSUED	SIGNATURE
NATDEFSERVMDL		17 OCT 1967	CO, 3rd RTBn RTR	JUN 1 1968	Bydi
VSM	w/1*	13Mar69	SECNAV	JUN 1 1968	McLeod CO
VCM	w/device	12Oct68	SECNAV		Long CO
CAR		690529	SECNAV		J.C. Crockett CO

TAYLOR, JAY L.

The President of the United States takes pleasure in presenting the BRONZE STAR MEDAL to

LANCE CORPORAL JAY L. TAYLOR

UNITED STATES MARINE CORPS

for service as set forth in the following

CITATION:

"For heroic achievement in connection with combat operations against the enemy in the Republic of Vietnam while serving as a Scout/Sniper with Headquarters Company, Seventh Marines, First Marine Division. On 28 March 1969, Lance Corporal Taylor, upon his own request, led a patrol of five other volunteers to an area in southeast Quang Nam Province in which he had previously sighted North Vietnamese Army soldiers moving along a well-used trail. Arriving at the designated location, he concealed his men in a tree line. Upon sighting several enemy soldiers moving along the trail some 900 meters distant, he alerted his men and directed their undetected movement across several hundred meters of open terrain to a position on a riverbank which intersected the enemy's route of approach. After skillfully deploying his men, he observed ten fully-armed enemy soldiers entering the water 300 meters down river in an attempt to reach the near bank. Although he realized that the target would be small once the hostile soldiers entered the water, Lance Corporal Taylor ordered his men to hold their fire until all ten of the enemy were in the river. Then, utilizing his Remington 700 sniper rifle, he began firing. Immediately, the hostile soldiers submerged and tried to evade the fire directed at them by the Marines by drifting down river. Disregarding the possibility of other enemy in the vicinity rushing to their comrades' aid, Lance Corporal Taylor took careful aim and killed 5 of the soldiers as they climbed the river bank now over 500 meters distant, and directed his men's fire upon three more at a closer range, thereby accouting for eight enemy killed. Lance Corporal Taylor's courage, bold initiative and unwavering devotion to duty at great personal risk contributed significantly to the accomplishment of his unit's mission and were in keeping with the highest traditions of the Marine Corps and of the United States Naval Service."

The Combat Distinguishing Device is authorized.

FOR THE PRESIDENT,

H. W. BUSE, JR.
LIEUTENANT GENERAL, U. S. MARINE CORPS
COMMANDING GENERAL, FLEET MARINE FORCE, PACIFIC

38. Forty Years Later

Captain Raymond Porter: I have not had any contact with Captain Porter since he left Vietnam. His parents, Mr. and Mrs. Porter, have both passed away. My mom saw Captain Porter at his mother's funeral a few years ago. He is now retired from the Marine Corps and I hope he is doing well.

Sergeant Mark Webb: Mark spent a total of thirty-one months in Vietnam. Mark was awarded the Purple Heart. After being discharged from the Marine Corps, he traveled to New Mexico to visit. Mark stayed, and we shared a rental house for a while. Mark met and married a wonderful woman. They had two boys, Jason and Jarred. Marks wife Pug is a school teacher, and Mark is now retired. He is an avid bow hunter. Mark is currently being treated for PTSD.

Pfc James Miller: James called me a few times after he first returned from Vietnam, but we have not had any contact now for over thirty years. My efforts to locate him have been unsuccessful thus far.

LCpl Colin McGee: Colin was wounded off of Hill 55 and was medevaced out of country. McGee and Foster were partners at the time and they had been sent out on a finger off of Hill 55 for three days in a row. The third day out they hit a booby trap and both sustained severe wounds. Colin is now retired from the Dearborn Police Department and is the manager of a retirement facility in Michigan. He also has a home in Florida where he and his wife enjoy spending time. Colin enjoys spending time with his grandchildren.

I had not had any contact with Colin until a year ago. It was great to hear him laugh again. I hope to see him soon.

Cpl John Perry: John was wounded and badly burned before leaving Vietnam when the amtrac he was riding hit a mine. He was awarded a Bronze Star while serving in Vietnam. When John returned to the States, he spent nine months recovering from his wounds. Upon returning home John married his childhood sweetheart Carol and they had four children. John now lives in Lima, Ohio, where he is a foundry manager.

I have only talked to John a few times in the last forty years, but we continue to exchange e-mails. Each year I visit Lexington, Kentucky, in September to attend the thoroughbred sale. Next year while I'm there, I plan to take a trip up to Ohio to visit with John.

Cpl William Martin: After forty years, Bill and I recently met again at the Scout Sniper Association reunion in San Diego, California. When McGee and Foster were hit, Bill was the first one to reach them. Bill and Stony were also with Rush and Babbyson when they were hit.

Bill was wounded twice while in Vietnam. The first time he was hit by two rounds in the chest, and fortunately his ammo bandoliers stopped the bullets. The second time he was not so lucky. On Mar 30, 1969, Bill sustained severe wounds to his legs when the grunt walking behind him tripped a booby trap. The grunt was mortally wounded. Bill spent six months in the hospital recovering from his wounds. He was then returned home and discharged from the Marine Corps.

Bill now lives in Arizona with his wife Jill. He owns his own construction company. Bill enjoyed drag racing and skydiving until recently. Now age and lingering problems from his wounds have slowed him down. Bill has been diagnosed with PTSD.

Cpl Robinson: Robbie was from Stockton, California, and had never left his hometown area until he joined the Marine Corps. Robbie served his first thirteen-month tour and one six-month extension. While on his thirty-day leave between tours Robbie purchased a new Corvette.

Robbie returned home and struggled with the memories of Vietnam. Robbie was Mott's team leader when he was killed, and like many who experienced similar ordeals, Robbie never completely forgave himself for Mott's death, even though there was nothing he could have done to prevent it.

After a failed marriage, Robbie traveled to New Mexico in 1971 and stayed with me for a couple of months. In 1987 I saw Robbie again while I was working in California. He was married and living in a cabin in the mountains outside of Sacramento, California. My attempts to locate Robbie again have been unsuccessful so far.

Cpl Ray Gonzales: Gunny was wounded in action in February 1969. Gunny completed his tour and extension in Vietnam in 1970. Two weeks after returning home, he was married. He and his wife had one son and two daughters. They have ten grandchildren and they are expecting their first great grandchild. Gunny worked in electronics for Corpus Christi Army Depot for thirty-five years and he is now retired and living in Corpus Christi, Texas. Gunny spends much of his time fishing.

SSgt James Gularte: Jim arrived in country July 1968 and rotated home in 1970. I had not heard from Jim for forty years. He returned to Vietnam after his ankle healed, but not to our unit. He was assigned to 1st Marine Division. Jim was injured three more times before leaving Vietnam. Jim and his wife Becky have been married for twenty years, and they have four children, two sons and two daughters.

I also met Jim again at the annual SSA reunion in San Diego. Jim is retired from the Oceanside Police Department. He also worked as a Federal air marshal for a while after he retired. He now volunteers much of his time to the Scout Sniper schools at Camp Pendleton, California, and in Hawaii. Jim's picture hangs on the wall at the Scout Sniper training center. He is the namesake of the Honor Graduates Trophy at the Camp Pendleton and 1st Marine Division Scout Sniper schools. He is the namesake of the High Shooter Award, Scout Sniper School USMC Base, Kaneohe Bay, Hawaii. He was recently awarded an Honorary Lifetime Membership AIT/SOI Instructors position at the Camp Pendleton and Hawaii Scout Sniper schools. It was a pleasure to have worked with Jim, and he is a credit to the Scout Sniper community and the Marine Corps.

Sgt Rick Rush: Rick spent nineteen months in country. He was wounded in February 1969 and never returned to the sniper platoon. Rick was eventually evacuated to Okinawa, where he recovered from his wounds. He then tried to extend in Nam for another six months, but when they would not guarantee he would be returned to the sniper platoon, he opted to rotate back to the States and was given an early out with nine months left in the Marine Corps.

Rick was a frequent user of recreational drugs during and after Vietnam, and at the Scout Sniper reunion I was glad to see Rick had changed his lifestyle. Rick now lives in Southern California and enjoys restoring antique cars and riding his Harley.

Cpl Charles Butler: Chuck was in country from September 1968 through October 1969. While Chuck was in Vietnam he lost two partners. There was absolutely nothing Chuck could have done to prevent the deaths of either one of his partners, and yet the thought, "What if I had done something different?" continues to haunt Chuck and will for the rest of his life. He now lives in Moores Hill, Indiana, with his wife Terry.

Chuck and Terry were also at the SSA reunion, and it was great to see Chuck again and meet his wife Terry. Chuck worked in the construction industry as a superintendent for a short time and owned his own construction business for many years. Chuck is now retired and is being treated for PTSD.

Cpl Lloyd Gomez: Lloyd spent thirty-four months in Vietnam. He extended four times. Lloyd and Chuck were partners in Nam for nine months. Eighteen years after returning from Vietnam, Charles Butler located Lloyd in his hometown of Alamosa, Colorado. They bought a hunting cabin together, and for the next fifteen years Chuck would travel to Colorado and visit Lloyd at least twice a year. They enjoyed hunting and spending time together in their cabin.

Lloyd Gomez passed away December 26, 2003. Lloyd's wife and family and Charles Butler were at his side. May he now rest in peace.

Cpl Timothy Pearson: I have just recently made telephone contact with Tim, and he is presently living in Bothell, Washington. After Tim left Vietnam he let his hair grow long and bought a motorcycle. Two years later he went back to school, earned his degree, and became an investment banker. In 1971 Tim met and married his wife, and they have one son. For the last sixteen years Tim has been a branch manager for a large bank in the Seattle area. I look forward to meeting Tim in person again.

LCpl Kogelman "Babbyson": Kogelman and Rick Rush were partners and were wounded at the same time. They had set up for the night when they were ordered to move. While picking up their gear, Kogelman tripped a bobby trap, wounding both of them and a grunt. Kogelman never returned to the Scout Sniper platoon. Shortly after returning home Kogelman committed suicide. May he rest in peace.

LCpl Larry Bridges: I never had a chance to talk to Larry after Vietnam, and he passed away four years ago. May he also rest in peace.

LCpl Lawrence J. Putz: Born January 16, 1949. Killed in action October 25, 1968. Putz had been in country only a short time when he sustained a fatal wound from an accidental discharge of a defective M-79. Chuck Butler was his team leader at the time.

Cpl Frederick L. Benishek: Born July 8, 1949. Killed in action June 6, 1969. Benishek was killed in a nighttime firefight when he sustained a gunshot wound to the head. Chuck Butler was his team leader at the time. Cpl Perry and his partner were with Butler and Benishek the night he was killed.

Pfc William Larry Mott: Born September 14, 1949. Killed in action January 29, 1969. After forty years, I finally managed to muster up the courage to visit Mott's mother in Jefferson City, Tennessee. On October 24, 2008, Chuck Butler and I walked up to Polly Mott's front door and rang the doorbell.

Cpl Jay Taylor: Like many returning vets, I struggled some after getting out of the Marine Corps. At the time I really didn't realize anything was wrong with me. Shellshock was a WWII condition, and PTSD had not yet surfaced as a disorder. I just wanted everything to be like it was before I left for Vietnam. I had no idea how much I had changed.

At first I could not sleep at night without a rifle or weapon of some sort in bed with me. Every night after Mom and Dad went to bed I would get up, take my 30.30 hunting rifle out of the closet, and place it beside me in bed. We had slept with our weapons for thirteen months in Vietnam, and it was a very hard habit to break. The nights were the worst. The dreams came at night. The fear of a night attack was still present, and the slightest noise would wake me up. I had always feared the nights in Nam; a bolt-action with a scope on it provided little protection at night. A sniper lost his advantage at night. I would wake early in the morning and put the rifle back in the closet so no one would know.

The war was very unpopular at the time, and no one wanted to talk about it. When I was around my old friends, they talked about school and the things they had been doing for the past year or so. I could only listen. Even though I wanted to talk about my experiences in Vietnam, I knew they would not understand, and it made them uncomfortable when I did talk about it.

My parents were just glad to have me back, and they too wanted everything to return to normal—don't talk about it and forget it ever happened. My mom took me to the doctor for a physical. I got an eye exam, a hearing test, and I had my teeth checked. Everything checked out fine—she had her boy back. Little did she know that the boy she sent off was never coming back. Going from a highly respected member of an elite unit in Vietnam back to a nineteen-year-old kid at home, with nothing in common with friends he had left behind, was a very difficult transition. I had the common symptoms of many returning vets—bad dreams, fear of crowds and loud noises, and a very bad and unpredictable temper that got worse as time went on.

I tried to go back to school. I enrolled in some classes at the University of New Mexico. I had been going to classes for less than a month when one evening while I was driving to school I heard on the radio where students were protesting on Central Avenue in front of the University. The announcer said that they were carrying antiwar signs and burning the American flag. The more I listened to it, the madder I got until I found myself wondering how many of them I could kill if I plowed into the crowd with my truck. I turned around and went back home. I knew if I continued to go to that university something bad was going to happen.

A short time later I got into an altercation with three young men at a car hop one night. One of the men pulled a knife and wanted to fight. I tried to walk away from the trouble and managed to get into my truck and back out into the street in an attempt to leave. As I was about to drive off, the one who had pulled the knife on me threw a two-foot-long piece of pipe through the front windshield of my truck. I snapped.

I carried an old Webley 38-caliber pistol in the glove box of my truck. I instantly had the pistol out and aimed at the young man, who upon seeing the pistol was off at a run. It was dark, but the light from the car hop allowed me to see him clearly. I intentionally missed with my first shot because I did not want to hit the nearby bystanders. The second round caught him right through the hinge of the jaw and dropped him like a rock. I thought I had killed him. I had wanted to kill him. If I could shoot a pistol as good as I could a rifle he would have been dead.

Luckily for me the young man I shot was wanted by the police for questioning involving an earlier incident. He survived the wound, and all charges against me were dropped. The whole incident worried me; I had come very close to killing someone and going to jail for a very long time. I now realized I could kill anybody—it didn't have to be a VC.

I went through a failed marriage. It was my attempt to be normal, get married, settle down, and maybe have kids. Unfortunately we both entered into the marriage for all of the wrong reasons, and after less than a year later we came to a mutual agreement: I was a bastard, she was a bitch, and we were divorced.

My solution to all of my problems was to drink and fight my way to happiness. Of course it didn't work very well, and it landed me in jail a number of times. Finally, after a few years I managed to pack all of my emotions concerning my Vietnam experience into a nice, neat pouch and store it away inside myself, and there it has remained until now.

In 1972 I traveled to Alaska, where I spent the next fourteen years. Alaska was good for me. Many of the people migrating to Alaska at the time were going to work on the pipeline. Some were just running away from their past. I seemed to fit in better with the people I met there; maybe it was because we had no common background. At the time, Alaska was still the last American frontier. The people there were friendly, and we helped each other.

I met my wonderful wife Paulette in Alaska, and we were married in 1979. We had two boys, Lee and Bobby. We have since moved back to New Mexico, where we currently live. My wife and I bought my parents' old home. We have also purchased a large portion of what used to be the Porter's apple orchard next door, where we raise thoroughbred racehorses. My mom is now eighty-four years young, and she lives across the street from us. My dad passed away six years ago.

I have worked for the same construction company, Hoffman Construction Company of Portland, Oregon, for the last thirty years as a project superintendent. Like many other Vietnam vets, including many of those with PTSD, I have managed to be a productive member of society as I continue to deal with my issues. Thanks to my kind and understanding wife, the dreams have gone away. Vietnam is now a lifetime ago. I also have been diagnosed with PTSD.

39. Epilogue

I would hope that now we are doing a better job of getting counseling for our men and women returning from combat and not just turning them loose in society without making an attempt to teach them coping skills.

Over the years, snipers have been portrayed as emotionless, stone-cold killers. For most of us nothing could be further from the truth. We were just doing our job, and most of us were very good at it. The trauma and events that hardened us then have diminish with time, but memories of what we did do not. I no longer hate the Vietnamese people. I have a great deal of respect for what they endured. As fighters they made the most of what they had and were a very formidable foe. I have also forgiven the American public and our government at the time for the way we were treated when we returned. We really were disposable warriors. I do regret that we did not receive the homecoming we so justly deserved.

I am concerned about whether or not I will be able to continue to deal with my emotional baggage as I grow older. Can I keep that bag of emotional garbage neatly tucked away and under control?

I strongly encourage all returning veterans to seek help immediately if they have unresolved issues or have experienced traumatic events while in combat. These are not issues any of us are qualified or able to deal with alone, and nor should anyone have to.

Last but certainly not least, I would like to dedicate this book to William L. Mott and all the others, on both sides, who never returned. May they never be forgotten.

References

1. www.marzone.com/7thMarines/Hst0001.htm
2. www.americal.org/firebase.shtml
3. greenmarine2002.com
4. www.rjsmith.com/kia_tbl.html
5. www.cia.gov/library/publications/the-world-factbook/geos/vm.html
6. www.marzone.com/7thMarines/Vn5500.htm
7. www.nexus.net/~911gfx/sea-ao.html
8. remembervietnam.homestead.com/mpcrvn.html
9. www.amervets.com/ssmedl.htm
10. www.macvsog.cc/statistics_about_the_vietnam_war.htm
11. www.militarymarksmanship.org/tapsmcmillan.htm
12. www.vietnam.ttu.edu/virtualarchive/
13. usmcscoutsniper.org/
14. usmcscoutsniper.org/join.htm
15. www.popasmoke.com/vietnam-war-facts.html
16. www.marzone.com/7thMarines/Faq0001.htm
17. www.3rdmarines.net/Vietnam_maps.htm
18. www.vietnamgear.com/casualties.aspx
19. www.ussboston.org/VietnamMyths.html
20. www.snowcrest.net/jmike/vietnammil.html
21. www.mrfa.org/vnstats.htm
22. www.war-stories.com/wall-search-1.asp
23. www.pjsinnam.com/VN_History/VN_War_Statistics.htm
24. www.thewall-usa.com/names.asp
25. www.fas.org/sgp/crs/natsec/RL32492.pdf
26. www.vhfcn.org/stat.htm

LaVergne, TN USA
14 September 2010
196886LV00001B/109/P